BORN
THIS FAE

Practical Wisdom and Guidance
from the Faery Realm to Live a
Vibrant and Prosperous Life

ERIN CHRISTINE

Born This Fae

ISBN: 979-8-9851186-0-5

Cover and Book Design by
Transcendent Publishing

TRANSCENDENT

The content of this book is for informational purposes only and is not intended to diagnose, treat, cure, or prevent any condition or disease. You understand that this book is not intended as a substitute for consultation with a licensed practitioner. Please consult with your own physician or healthcare specialist regarding the suggestions and recommendations made in this book. The use of this book implies your acceptance of this disclaimer.

Printed in the United States of America.

DEDICATION

To every female voice ever silenced, stifled, or scorned.
May the fire of your truth set you free.

CONTENTS

INTRODUCTION

I have spent the last twenty-six years turning over curious stones, peeking around dark corners, seeking answers to questions I had no words for, and looking for the sweet something that I knew had to be somewhere along this path I was on. I was being led towards something, that's for sure, but I had only a pocket full of mismatched clues to go on. Yet I continued to wander into the unknown, and with each new sunrise I was shown a bit more, until one day I woke up and realized that the answers I'd been searching for were inside of me all along. I could no longer deny the presence of a higher power at work in my life. I had come face to face with my soul. In that moment, I knew without a doubt that I was here on assignment to teach and learn love. But now what?

I grew up as the daughter of a real-life magician. I am talking about a lighthearted, jovial man with a paunch belly and a smile that beamed out of his eyes, who could stand on a stage, incite an audience to uncontrollable belly laughs and wow them with curious card tricks, colorful mysteries, and sleight of hand. He came alive on that stage. This was his magic. But when the curtain went down and the lights dimmed, he swirled into a dark, angry shadow of a man that I learned very early on to fear. It was this fear, I later learned, that was my first real lesson in learning to love.

I have spent a lifetime trying to make sense of a world I could not fit into. A storyteller, empath, poet and magician, I move through it breathing in a balance of human suffering and alchemy. But growing up, I only understood the pain. I was the proverbial black sheep in my family, always in trouble, constantly being criticized for something. I am a deeply feeling person and viewed life through a unique lens that even I did not understand. I only wanted to be loved and accepted in my family, but it seemed everything I said or did was filtered through a lens of fear and control, creating toxic situations steeped in belittlement, blame, and at times, leading to physical violence.

Yet, in the midst of all the pain and confusion, there was also a mysterious undercurrent weaving its way through me. My mom would always tell me about my maternal grand-mother, and how "she just knows things." She never said anything more than that, but I couldn't help but feel my grandmother was a magical being, even though I had no idea what that even meant. I also had a fondness for being outdoors and collecting various elements of nature such as rocks, sticks, and bundles of flowers. It wasn't unusual to see me come home from a friend's house covered in mud. We had a huge china-berry tree on our side yard, and even though my mom was always after me and my sister about how poisonous the berries were, it became my second home. In the spring of 2002 Spirit woke me up – a cosmic, kaleidoscopic experience of color, sight, and sound that left me thinking I was losing my mind. But suddenly I was seeing things in a brand-new way, hearing voices and sounds I'd never heard before, and feeling beautiful sensations in my body that I couldn't fully explain. And oddly enough, life began to make sense, though not in the usual way. It was a feeling deep down in my bones that I had been here before… a knowing, a truth. And even though I had no idea what to make of all of this, I knew it was leading somewhere magical.

In order to experience the magic of this world, you must be willing to believe it exists, even if you think you're crazy! I *still* think I am, and I've been working with my spirit guides for almost twenty years now. But this is the truth as I know it – I've seen and experienced too much to believe otherwise. My guides delivered my wake-up call directly, though they did not descend from the heavens as I anticipated they would. Well, not exactly. My guides came from the earth. I will introduce you to them in the coming chapters, for now, I'll just say that working with them has changed my life in beautiful, unimaginable ways; in fact, I can hardly remember the person I was prior to meeting them. They taught me how to communicate with nature, how to connect deeply with all of life, and how to tune into my body and use it as a magic wand. Yes, it's true, and you can do the same! You have the power and presence within you to create your own miracles every day, and I'm going to show you how!

Since that awakening, Spirit has taken me on journey after journey, guiding me, teaching me, picking me up every time I fall, and showing me how to be the best version of myself so that I can help create a healthier, more beautiful planet for all of us. This book is a remembering of who I am underneath the blood and the bones. These words are a reclamation of my power, my presence, and my purpose in this world. This is my coming-out party, shaking off the fear of my spiritual gifts and unpacking my voice from a lifetime of silence.

This book is also for you, dear reader. I see you. I feel your heart. You too struggle, trying to make sense of a world you don't fit into. I know you've seen some dark times and pulled yourself out of deep, heavy places. I know you feel things down to your bones, things you don't talk about. I see you, and this book is *for* you. My words are for you. I share my stories here to inspire you to share yours. Your voice matters. Your pain matters. There are people out in the world praying to connect with someone like you, someone who has gone through the things you've experienced. Through my stories and experiences, I will share with you tools and techniques that my guides taught me. It is my hope to open your heart to a realm of possibility, magical possibility that is available to all of us if we only ask. It is my hope to inspire you to look on this world and your life with new eyes. Being human is really fucking hard! Spirit is here to help guide us so that we can smooth the edges of life and enjoy the ride more. I am here to lift you up, help you find your brave, and celebrate your unique imprint in this world.

It is my hope that after reading this, you will have the courage to face your deepest, darkest fears, reacquaint yourself with your true nature, and build and/or strengthen your relationship with Mother Earth.

FAERY AWAKENING

It was March of 2002, and I was sitting across from a tiny, ethereal woman named Jenny. She had delicate features and blond hair that hung down past her waist. She said she was an angel reader, but I'll be darned if she didn't look just like an angel herself! I spent an hour with her while she relayed things to me from the angelic realm. Some of her words resonated deeply inside my being, while others just seemed too much for me to believe.

At one point during the session, she said to me, "You have faeries flying all around you!" She then went on to tell me that faeries are angelic messengers that watch over the planet and all Her elements. They are the keepers of our land, bodies of water, plant life, and animal life — basically anything in the natural world is protected and nurtured by the faery realm. And because I was very pregnant at the time, she mentioned that the faery realm also watched over the children of this world. Jenny then gave me a list of books and meditation CDs to help me learn how to connect with the angels and faeries on my own. I really didn't know what to think of this woman and all she had shared with me, but I floated out of her office feeling strangely euphoric and dreamy.

One week later I was sitting on the patio in my backyard, headphones on, ready to embark on my very first guided

1

meditation experience. I had no expectations, but I was over-thinking everything! I closed my eyes and just let myself listen to the soothing voice and curious words. I surprised myself by falling into a deeply relaxed state. When the meditation ended, I sat there for a long moment just breathing in the bliss I felt. This was a new feeling for me!

I opened my eyes and stared into my backyard. It looked cloudy and alive, almost like a wave of water was washing over the entire yard and I could see right through it to the other side. For what felt like several minutes I just stared off into space, filled with a peace I had never felt before, and that's when it happened! It was as if someone had taken a large orange Home Depot bucket filled with gold glitter and threw it right at my face. Gold flecks filled the air, and I didn't dare breathe. I just stared, wide-eyed, watching them flutter around me. Suddenly, they showed themselves. The flittering gold began to take shape until I saw tiny, iridescent bodies with shimmery wings surrounding me. What on earth was happening? Was I really seeing what I thought I was seeing? If I closed my eyes, would they still be there when I opened them? I didn't want this beautiful magic to end, but I had to know. So, for one long moment, I squeezed my eyes shut. I took in a deep breath and opened them again. The shimmering figures remained. I didn't know it in that moment, but I had just met my spirit guides.

It has been nearly two decades since this experience, and my guides have remained ever-present, active participants in my life. They've taught me the language of nature, the ebb and flow of change, and how to connect deeply with all of life. In fact, the more I worked with my guides, the less human I felt.

It was as if I was being born into another world, as if my DNA was changing with each passing day. Sharing this message with you is my promise to them, my gift back to God, to help protect and honor Mother Earth. In the pages that follow, I am going to take you on a magical journey into some of the deepest parts of nature. With an open heart and a willing mind, you will see just how simple and easy it is to connect to the energy of the fae.

Meet Your Guide

Are you ready to meet your spirit guide? Find a quiet place to sit or lay down comfortably where you will not be disturbed. An outside location is best, but if you find yourself indoors, situate yourself near a plant or picture of a nature scene. You can also use your pet or photograph of pets as a focal point. Begin by closing your eyes and taking in three or four slow, deep breaths, in through your nose for a count of three, then out through your mouth for a count of four. Allow your breathing to flow naturally as you feel your body begin to relax. At this point, you can either keep your eyes closed, or open them to focus on the plant or picture that you've chosen. Allow yourself to look beyond the object. You will notice your gaze begin to soften, becoming hazy. You might start to see bright colors or lights floating across your line of sight. You may even begin to see images or snapshots of faces. Just allow for all this to pass through your presence. If you start to question your visions, you will break the flow of energy coming through you.

This is not a time to judge or question what you're experiencing. Let it all flow. You are a witness and nothing more.

It is now time to invite your guide to come to you. There is no wrong way to do this, so do not worry about trying to find the perfect words. Your guides have been waiting to hear from you and need only your permission to enter your world. Your invitation can be as simple as, "Beloved Guides, please come to me now." This can be done as a heartfelt mental request. Nature will hear you; I promise. Your thoughts are that powerful! Do your best to remain a witness to your experience so as not to question whatever arises. If you find yourself overthinking your request or the attachment to the result, gently bring yourself back to stillness with your breath. You were born connected to source energy. You cannot mess this up. Another way to reach out is to call on each of the different elements. Simply think the words, "Faeries of the wind, faeries of the flame, faeries of the water, faeries of the earth." Unbeknownst to me when I first connected with my faery guides, the ones who show up for you may be connected to your astrological sun sign. I am an Aquarian, which is an air sign, and my guides are faeries of the wind. This doesn't mean that you won't connect with the other elements, but it'll give you clues to help you become clearer on who is trying to connect with you. Discernment is key! As you go deeper into this work, you will begin to connect with the other elements as you are ready. Each element feels different, just like they do in real life. You will begin to feel the unique spiritual nuances of each as you progress. Think about your favorite place to spend time in nature. For example, if you happen to love the beach, you may find yourself connecting easily with water faeries. Your guides have been with you since birth. There's a reason you resonate with specific places like this. This journey you are on is much like a five-thousand-piece kaleidoscope puzzle, with Spirit speaking in tiny pieces. It is important to keep track of it all so that, over time, you can begin to see the bigger picture. Get yourself a journal or notebook and start writing down your experiences. Pay attention! Nature is subtle, and even the most seemingly trivial encounters are part of your evolution. This is how you learn the language of nature. Nature will speak to you in a way that only you can understand. They will give you only what you are ready for. I will offer you this caveat: if you are like me and need to know everything all at once, be careful what you ask for.

You are in a very relaxed state by now. You've invited your guides to join you. Trust that they heard you. This is important! In this relaxed place, you are open and receptive to spirit communication. Just allow. Whatever comes in, just notice it. You will record everything as soon as you are finished, so do not worry too much about trying to remember everything now. Whatever is for you in this moment will remain in your memory. Now this is when it gets really fun! There are infinite ways nature will let you know of their presence in your life. In this space it's not uncommon to see animals, plants, or insects flash across your mental movie screen. You may also see people, never-before-seen scenarios playing out like a movie, or numbers and symbols. Past memories may also surface. If this is occurring, your clairvoyance or spiritual vision is opening up. You may also hear voices and/or sounds. These can come through audibly as if someone is speaking to you directly or telepathically, which sounds like your own thoughts. Telepathy can be tricky to discern because you have to trust yourself that these new thoughts are communication from Spirit. When this happens, your clairaudience or spiritual hearing is awakening. Another way you may experience your guides speaking to you is through clairsentience, or a clear feeling moving through your body. This has been a curious feeling to work through myself. I remember sitting with a client and hearing myself say, "I'm feeling like I'm seeing an ice cream cone." I wasn't actually seeing an ice cream cone, but I had this feeling like I was experiencing the sight of one. As strange as this statement sounded to me, Spirit knew it was exactly what she needed to hear and ended up creating a light bulb moment for her healing process in our session.

The Voice

Nature speaks in limitless ways. It can be very frustrating in the beginning, when you are trying to make sense of all the sensory input. This is why it is so important to make a point to connect regularly and record as much as possible in your journal. Much like yoga, it must become a practice in order for you to see and experience the true beauty of what's being offered to you. I'm at a point now where I'm in contact all day, every day. It's my lifeline. It's how I make sense of a world filled with pain and fear. But the voice you hear one day may not be the same voice you hear the next. Nature speaks in a collective voice, as well as individually, depending on the element coming through.

When you are learning to discern the language, you will hear either audibly or telepathically words like "us" or "we." This is a clue that the collective is speaking. However, it can also be the voice of a single group of energies, such as bees. This is where your connection and conversation come in handy. Ask questions, like *Who is speaking to me now? Who is this trying to get my attention?* Again, don't overthink this. Your guides already know you're there. They know your thoughts before you even complete them in your mind. Simple language from an open, sincere heart is all you need to make connection. When you hear language using "I" or "me" then you can confirm that a single energy is speaking to you. When you ask your questions, tune into your body. Pay attention to any feelings or sensations that may be moving through you. Do not discount anything. Just notice and record in your journal as soon as possible. Some of the sensations you may feel are goosebumps, flutters of energy around your head and face, twitches, you may also feel this immense love move through your body. There is no mistaking it! You will truly feel like you are sitting on a cloud in heaven. Truth is, you are. Heaven on earth is created by us, through us, when we have the courage to surrender our control and connect to our source energy. It's in these gentle moments that miracles begin to take shape in our lives. This is how we heal our hearts from a lifetime of hurts and begin to create a magical life that excites and inspires us. You may also see visions, symbols, or colors when you connect, much like when you reached out to meet your guide. This is nothing to fear. I assure you your eyes are fine. Your spiritual sight is opening and expanding, and you are now seeing the different layers of consciousness. This is reason to celebrate! It takes immense courage to surrender the rigid religion and early conditioning that has clouded our connection to the very source that gives us life.

Reverence

Something extraordinary happens when you begin to connect with nature. You begin to see the world with brand new eyes. Colors are brighter, scents and sounds are sweeter. Everything feels healthy and alive, and you can feel this energy move through your body. When this happens, you start to feel a deep appreciation for the planet as a whole. All of life becomes sacred and worthy of great respect. In the early years, I found myself really connecting with insects and bugs. I remember one day in the spring of 2002, just after my wake-up call. At the time I was teaching kindergarten in South Phoenix, and as I was leading my students back from their art class, I suddenly noticed a caterpillar scooting his way across the sidewalk. I was so happy to see this so I gathered the kids around so they could watch him too. As we all stood there huddled around this little guy, one of my boys stepped out of the circle and slammed his foot down on the caterpillar, crushing it instantly. The intensity of the emotions I felt took me by complete surprise. I was so sad at the creature's death that I wanted to cry, and so angry at this little boy for killing it that I wanted to hurt him so he could feel what it was like. These thoughts and feelings scared me, and of course I would never hurt a child, but in the moment they were overwhelming. I also realized, though, that the boy was just doing what he'd done all along, what he had seen his parents do. Like most of us, he was raised to think that bugs were a nuisance and something to just get rid of. We mindlessly squash spiders, insects, and bugs whenever they appear. It is considered normal. Once upon a time it was my normal too. But something inside of me was changing and this was the start of it.

Faeries and humans have struggled for millennia to coexist. As humans plodded forth in pursuit of progress and expansion, faeries were left to watch as the planet took hit after hit to its natural resources. This caused faeries to become angry and skeptical of humans, and rightfully so. Could you love or trust someone destroying the very thing you'd worked so hard to cultivate and preserve, the very thing we all need to survive? Faeries want to be seen, honored, and allowed to care for this earth alongside the people who inhabit Her. But their anger and distrust towards humans keeps them hidden, except to those who seek them out and commit to their cause. It's really *everyone's* cause. This is our planet, and it's the responsibility of each of us to take care of Her. But we need only look outside or turn on the evening news to see that that is not happening. Incredible planetary destruction is occurring as we speak. Many times, faeries are looked on as tricksters, troublemakers, or even devils incarnate. They truly want to know and love humans but have a hard time because they cannot let go of their anger. They want to trust that we humans are going to do our job and take good care of our planet, but we keep messing that up. (We are human, after all). Faeries will play tricks on people to get our attention. They may hide things of yours, move things around your house, or cause you to have minor accidents. If things like this are happening in your world, instead of getting frustrated or angry, get curious. You may have a faery guide shaking up your world to get your attention; if so, you've been called to do this work. It could be an answer to a prayer of yours, or part of your soul's purpose. It will be one of the most challenging endeavors you will ever encounter, and at the same time, you will experience a life so vibrant and beautiful. You will fall in love with your life, experience the magic of yourself, and live every day on purpose, creating a happier, healthier planet for us all. Your life will never be the same.

Coming Out of Hiding

Connecting with the faery realm is a wondrous and fantastic experience. I remember in the early days feeling so alive with possibility. I was seeing mystical creations materialize daily. I felt like I would burst with excitement if I didn't tell people about my encounters, yet I kept them to myself. I had been ridiculed my entire life for thinking differently and I wasn't about to start giving people a reason to judge me further. Instead, this new realm became my magical escape. There was a park near my house that I would walk to every day and spend hours swinging high on the swings and letting my thoughts wander into their world. When I returned home I would journal everything I could remember. I had a really hard time trusting what I was experiencing, especially since most of what came through was telepathy and sounded just like my own thoughts. I struggled with this a lot. I am a need-to-know person and I had so many questions. How could I be sure what I was getting was from Spirit? The more I invited my guides in for conversation, the more I noticed patterns in their words and how they made me feel inside. The energy of their words was always very gentle and uplifting not at all like the mean girl inner critic who ran her mouth off inside of me each day. Even if they were telling me something I needed to change or work on, it was always delivered with kindness, a gentle, loving support that I'd never experienced before. And

11

over time, I began to feel their words in my body. First it was the goosebumps that started at the top of my head and traveled down my entire body. I knew something magical was happening the day I felt them on my cheeks! Then I would feel this warmth, coupled with an inner peace that oozed out of my every pore. I just felt so good, so at ease with myself. Even if I had completely lost my mind and was making all this up, there was no denying the love I felt flowing through my body. Whatever was happening, I was without a doubt, one hundred percent on board.

If you feel like you are still peeking out of the spiritual closet, it is important to find your tribe of people, your inner circle, a sacred support system where you are free to be and express however you need to. Not only will you receive the support you need, you will also be a source of support for others. As you begin to connect more with nature, you will also start to connect more deeply with yourself. When this happens, you are tapping into your own source power. This is the power that allows you to create your world in a way that is pleasing to you and feels in alignment with the direction you are wanting to go. What this means is that you are not going to have to look very far or work too hard to find these people who are ready to love you exactly as you are. If you pay attention, Spirit will lead you right to the perfect places and opportunities. You will cross paths with people who are just like you. You will recognize them by how they feel, their vibe. That same love you feel when you connect with nature is the same feeling you will feel among people who are like you. Get to know this feeling! Tuning in to your body this way allows you to build trust in yourself. It is this trust that will give you the courage and discernment to navigate any situation life brings you with knowingness and grace. It will also help you know when a person or situation is not for your highest good. You will also notice that your tribe speaks the same language as you do, the language of energy, vibration, of nature. You need not worry about not understanding them, you are fluent! This is the language of your cellular being, it is encoded in your DNA. This awareness for you is simply a remembering of who you are, which is a child of God, always connected to source energy.

This can be a very exciting time as you step into your truth; however, it can also be a challenging and confusing time. As you grow your spiritual family, you may notice your other friends and family members begin to treat you differently. They may question or criticize your new friends. They may speak or act differently around you or pull away; they may even break off all contact. As painful as this feels, it is actually a normal and natural response to your expansion. You are growing and learning things that light you up, but it can trigger people who do not understand or feel fear towards what you are experiencing. You are changing for the better and not everyone is ready to see or accept that. This is why your tribe is so important. You will need them to help you move through the pain of disappointing friends and family, or losing them altogether. On the other hand, you may be the one to release them. You will understand that not everyone can walk this new path with you. This is another indication of your incredible growth, and a gift to you both, even if it does not feel that way in the moment. Just as you cannot reach your highest potential with attachments that do not serve you, neither can they.

Imagine if you were taking a boat trip to a magical island paradise. You arrive at the dock with every suitcase you own containing every piece of clothing in your closet. The captain says you must leave behind half of what you've brought because the extra weight will keep the boat from operating. Are you going to pass up your opportunity to travel to this once-in-a-lifetime destination? Of course not! You will release the extra items because you know it is for the best. This is what happens on the road to truth. You have the opportunity to experience total freedom within yourself, but it is going to cost you some friends and family. It is a harsh reality, but as you cultivate a deeper understanding of the direction of your life it will be easier to forgive situations and see the broken relationships through eyes of love. You will absolutely grieve their loss. You will feel the pain of rejection, disappointment, betrayal. Let it all burn through your body. Cry it out, rage if you have to, just give it permission to move through and out of you. By fully allowing yourself to feel whatever emotions come up, you will process the experience much faster, bringing yourself that much closer to the highest expression of yourself.

The path to your highest self is fraught with pain, grief, incredible heartbreak, and loss. But it also is the most loving, authentic, supportive journey you will ever travel. Take heart, my friend, you must go! Your soul is calling.

LIFE AS AN EMPATH

It wasn't until recently, maybe the last three to five years, that I noticed the word empath popping up all over the place. The writers would list all these qualities that they felt defined a person as an empath. I could feel each word down to my bones: highly intuitive, introverted, highly sensitive, strong connection to nature and animals, "that" person everyone told their problems to, overwhelmed in large, crowded areas, suffers from chronic fatigue and/or pain, tendency to absorb others' emotions, and many, many more. Being an empath is a deeply felt journey into the depths of self, a painful, confusing dark walk of the soul. It is also a beautiful, inspiring ocean of art and humanity. Being an empath is magnificence and grace personified.

One of the most powerful things I uncovered during this journey is my insatiable desire to help people. There are few things harder for me than seeing people in pain. I feel it, I know it, and all I want to do is take it away from them so they can be at peace. This awareness of self is what has taught me the most about being an empath, being of service in this life, and knowing how to manage my own boundaries.

During the summer of 2012 I experienced a huge shift in perception about myself and my place in this world. It came to me in a dream. *As I stood on the edge, looking over the gaping hole that had all but consumed the planet, I realized I had a purpose, a calling that had lived within my core so deep and now was coming forth for me to acknowledge. I peered into the darkness and could hear in their cries the despair and fear that people had allowed to take over their lives. I reached down into the nothingness and felt someone grab my hand. I held onto this person until they were able to climb out and stand in the light with me. Again and again, I reached down to feel hands grabbing at mine, trying to reach the light.*

I woke from the dream in a complete state of awe. I knew what I had to do, but I had not one clue as to how it would happen. I am a bringer of light, a lightworker, a wayshower. They all basically mean the same thing. I am here to help people raise their consciousness to a higher level so that as a planet we begin to tip the scales in favor of the light, instead of focusing on the darkness. When I say darkness, I'm referring to all the fear that permeates our planet. We are bombarded with it every day – murders, rapes, wars, environmental catastrophes, government breakdowns – coming through our phones, computers and TVs. All of it is brought on by fear. My dream showed me that I am here to be of service to the world by teaching people how to love unconditionally. I was literally lifting people into the light. When they stood on the edge beside me, they were fearless.

This knowingness felt overwhelming! Why me? How much could one person help? Where and how was I supposed to begin? But Spirit never drops the ball; if a calling has been laid on your heart, you can bet your life you will be shown the way. I began to meditate daily – not an easy thing for a recovering Type A personality and proud workaholic. But over time, it became my daily solace. My faeries were always standing by with information to help me better understand my purpose and my responsibility to it. *You have a very important job to do here on the planet, my dear. It will not be easy. But you are a warrior spirit and we have complete faith in your capabilities. You do too, because you chose this assignment. Your purpose is to teach the people of this world about us. Again, it will not be easy. We will guide you every step of the way. You must listen. The planet is in grave danger. Humans have allowed for too long the destruction and over-consumption to take over and it is time to stop. It must if we are to continue living as we do on this planet.*

Now I don't know about you, but I was more than a little freaked out about the fact that it was my purpose to teach the world about faeries. Wasn't there anyone else who could do it? Who would believe me? Would they laugh at me? Call me crazy? Who knew? I could not wrap my brain around this idea. How would I even go about it? But again, I was asked to trust the process and just begin. I have since learned that it's not my job to convince others of anything in this life. This work brings me great joy and satisfaction, making it easy for me to share openly about it. My responsibility lies only in being true to myself and the gifts that God has built into my heart. I teach those who see themselves in me. I teach those who are ready to see beyond their physical experience. I teach so that I may be free, allowing my voice to wave out into the world for others who are looking for answers to their deepest questions. Ultimately, the faery realm is simply a gateway to God. Jesus is a gateway to God; Buddha is a gateway as well. Mother Mary, the Archangels, even your ancestors are all gateways to God. We are multidimensional beings able to transcend all levels of consciousness and connect to Source at any given time. We need only tune in. We are born to manifest the greatness of our Divine Creator. It is up to us to embrace that, quirks and all, and allow our light to shine out into the world.

Of course, in order to help people alleviate their pain, I would have to know what it felt like, and unbeknownst to me, I was about to experience some of the most incredible pain imaginable. This felt like an initiation of sorts, a crash course into the life of an empath. I've since learned that part of my purpose here in this life is to alchemize pain for the entire planet. This means that my body is used as a vessel to transmute pain and fear into light and love, then return it to Source or send back out to blanket the planet. Any time something occurs on this planet, be it local to me, or across the world, I will feel it in my body.

During the time leading up to the 2020 election, which overlapped with the surge of Covid-19, there was so much fear and stress attacking the planet I could hardly leave my house. Even a simple trip to the grocery store had the potential to land me in bed the rest of the day. Think about how you feel when you walk into a place with a very dense, fear-based vibe. Bars are famous for this! Alcohol lowers a person's vibration drastically. If they already operate on the lower end of the scale, adding alcohol just makes it worse. The important thing to note here is that every person on the planet feels these energies to some degree. But not everyone is aware of them, and if they are they may not be able or willing to manage them.

So how does a person move through life like this, feeling the intensity of everyone's vibrational baggage? How does one make sense of a world that hurts like hell to even be a part of? It's important to start seeing your life as a practice, a daily meal of rituals, routines, and activities that you live by. As with any practice, it takes time and immense patience to develop. You've heard before that your life is a journey. There is no such thing as a one-and-done fix for any of your pains and ailments. The roots of our beings run deep, creating a network of awareness, healing, and integration that remains with us our entire lives. You are on this path to cultivate your practice, to weave the magic that makes your life meaningful, enjoyable, and sustainable and, in doing so, bring great healing, joy, and purpose to the entire planet. So where do we start? There are specific things that the body needs on a regular basis to operate optimally – vibrant healthy food free of chemicals, movement, time spent in nature, plenty of rest, and sunshine. These seem like no-brainers, so it's surprising how many of us do not provide them for ourselves, myself included. I live in a very dry, excessively hot climate, so there are many months I don't get outside as much as I need to, and I notice the difference. I become sluggish, irritable, and restless. If you find yourself in a similar situation and are looking for a place to start, this is it. A daily walk, even just around your neighborhood, can do wonders for the body and spirit. If you already have exercise routines in place, consider moving them outdoors and see if that doesn't increase your energy levels and enjoyment. It's important to note that it does not matter how you move your body, only that you do so on a regular basis. If you are engaging in movement that brings you joy, you will have a much easier time sustaining the activity over time. And if you're not sure what you would enjoy doing, think play! Think fun! Think back to your childhood when you spent hours outside without a care in the world. Traveling back to those days will give you clues as to what lights you up.

Another great place to begin is by changing up your food choices. This is a super simple way to raise your vibration, but it can be difficult, especially if you have struggled with weight issues, eating disorders, or any traumatic experiences attached to food. Make it easier on yourself by choosing one fruit or vegetable you eat on a regular basis and swapping it out for the organic variety, then do more when you feel you can. When it feels good, maybe swap out an entire recipe for organic ingredients. The beauty in doing this work is to move with the flow of your being. I can tell you all the things that have worked for me, but if they are not resonating with you, honor that. We are here to enjoy our lives, so making choices that nurture that is what is important. You know better than anyone what is best for you in each moment. The themes in this book are here to remind you of the power you hold and help you tune into it and learn how to trust it.

So what happens when you find yourself dealing with unexplained illness or pain in your body? I spent almost fifteen years of my life as a competitive bodybuilder. I was doing all the things I discuss above, but like anyone I still experienced the occasional pain in my body. But when it started showing up more often and sticking around for longer periods, I began to wonder. The pain centered mainly on my low back and hips, sometimes moving up both sides of my abdominals and wrapping around my pelvic region. It vacillated between direct, sharp shooting pain on my lower lumbar spine and deep pelvic cramps that felt like I was in labor. At times I was consumed by both. I felt like a prisoner of this pain. I couldn't move, I couldn't work, I could barely breathe. It would take me years to understand what was actually happening: the process of alchemizing pain for the world, that I mentioned earlier. Spirit was taking me through my training, and because I knew in my being that I had signed up for this mission I had no choice but to allow it to consume me.

In the early days of this pain, it would flare up out of the blue during a work shift or workout. People would ask me, "What did you do?" and though I did not believe that I had done anything to injure myself, I would satisfy their curiosity by saying, "Oh I must have pulled a muscle at work or worked out too hard." The pain would last a day or two and then things would go back to normal. However, as I mentioned, this started happening more often and was now persisting for an average of five to seven days. It was definitely getting worse and I still had no idea what was happening. I considered myself a very healthy woman, and aside from working out more than most, there was no viable reason for me to be in such pain. Over time, these spells became exhausting. I was frustrated, angry, and desperate for peace in my body. I also had a very real fear of western medicine, so I had not been to any doctor to have this checked out. I believed so strongly in my body's innate healing capabilities that I put all my energy into self-healing. I prayed fiercely. I was angry at my body for what felt like the ultimate betrayal. When the pain literally brought me to my knees, I had no choice but to surrender. I began to talk to my body, much like I was getting to know a new friend – asking questions and holding space in stillness for the answers. It was during these desperate pleas to my body that I learned she hears our every thought and every word we utter; she feels our vibration, and she responds. This is the universal intelligence, the Holy Spirit, the higher self, moving through our being. This realization was the beginning of the beautiful, symbiotic relationship that I now have with my body and the spirit that moves through her and connects us both in deep, soul-searching love.

Eventually, I was speaking to my body on a regular basis. We were like old friends sitting on the porch with a glass of wine, safe in the knowing of our deepest connection, laughing at our foibles, embracing the memories. Yet the pain was still showing up on a monthly basis and I was missing so much work I feared I would lose my job. There is no greater fear for a single mama than thinking you might lose your sole financial support, but there was nothing I could do but surrender and trust. Surrender and trust are still two of the most challenging concepts for me to embrace. I imagine they are for you as well. But I began to notice curious patterns in my pain, specifically the timing of when it would show up. I would have flare-ups during my moon cycle each month, as well as any grand planetary shifts such as Mercury Retrograde, full moons, new moons, solar flare storms, et cetera. These planetary shifts are natural, normal parts of our collective evolution, so each time they occur, everyone on the planet is tuned in to the energy of the movement, each affected in their own unique way. Our healing journeys are all different and yet all for the collective good. These planetary shifts meet us wherever we are. Watching these patterns play out in my world only made things more challenging in some ways. I knew that my consciousness was expanding and evolving, yet I still had to go to work and be normal. How does one be normal when it feels like your human DNA is being replaced with something crystalline, something that vibrates at such a high rate you barely understand it yourself? Now, when someone asked what I had done to hurt my back, I would shrug my shoulders and say, "It's just doing its thing." I did not know how to respond in a way that people would understand. This bothered me at first, but over time I began to accept myself and my pain as part of my beautiful journey. It is incredibly liberating to release attachment to others' thoughts and opinions. I also learned that I had to release my attachment to speaking to be understood. Not that I wouldn't clarify if someone had questions or curiosity about what I was sharing, but I could no longer water myself down for the comfort of others. Not only was it exhausting, but it also kept me from being in the highest state of my own vibration. This is the core of the quote, "Be the change you wish to see in the world."

When we take responsibility for our own healing and shift our vibration into higher, more evolved states, we automatically send that vibration out into the world. That higher consciousness then has no choice but to blanket the earth, and the souls who are vibrating in sync with our vibration will feel it and begin to gravitate towards us or others who hold that same vibration. This is why we need people to shine the brightest light they can. What benefits one, benefits all. We are all responsible for the healing and regeneration of this planet, every single one of us. When we do this, we can finally lay to rest the thought of "I'm just one person, what good can I possibly do?" Hear this, my friend, you are not a small and insignificant random occurrence on this planet. You are a living, breathing miracle of love and light and your energy is needed so very deeply right now. You have enormous power to effect global change. You simply need to decide and allow for your light to shine out into the world. The Universe takes care of the rest.

One of the best ways I learned more about energy and vibration was through Reiki training. My journey with Reiki began in 2004, when I received my Level I and II certification. I went on to receive my master/teacher attunement in 2012. Reiki, a Japanese healing modality that channels life force energy, or chi, through the hands, can heal a person on all levels. A Reiki practitioner or Master Teacher attunes the student to sacred symbols that are placed into the auric field. Reiki is noninvasive, and creates a deep sense of peace and relaxation. When this happens the body will automatically drop into its innate healing space and create movement of anything that is causing energetic blocks, such as toxic thought patterns or behaviors, perhaps something from old childhood conditioning. The block could also be connected to an energetic attachment to a person who no longer serves your greatest good or doesn't have your best interest at heart.

Reiki is a beautiful way to get to know your body on a deeper level. When you allow yourself to drift into stillness and give yourself permission to just be, you create the space for your body to speak to you in its energetic language. As you learn this language, you will be able to hear your heart clearly and make decisions based on your highest good, rather than something old and toxic that's been holding you back. It's not a religion or belief system. You need only be willing to receive for Reiki to do its magic.

Now, let's talk about boundaries! This is one of the most important sections in this book, so read it carefully, multiple times if you must. We cannot be our best selves without boundaries. We simply cannot. As energetic beings, we are constantly in a state of mixing and melding with other energies. It's unavoidable. We merge with our family, our friends, our colleagues and coworkers, even strangers on the street. When we become aware of our own energy and vibration, we begin to notice the different vibes that people operate from. An angry vibe clearly feels much different than that of someone who's feeling happy and content. Each emotion has a different frequency. Shame and guilt have the lowest vibrations on the energetic spectrum – even anger, which is also considered low vibration, is considerably higher than them. Anger is higher than fear as well. As you begin to heal and become aware of all the different vibes, you may not necessarily be able to distinguish your vibe from that of others; you just know something feels off. It takes time to learn how to discern what you're feeling, and requires you to get in touch deeply with your body so you can access your emotions.

It's important to create a loving intimate relationship with your emotions. When you do this, you are showing yourself unconditional love. Loving and accepting your emotions, even all the uncomfortable ones, gives you the power to love and accept the emotions of others. And when you can do this, magic happens! You can now respond lovingly when triggered instead of reacting from a place of woundedness. Loving and accepting your emotions also means knowing and understanding that you are not going to be in a high, happy vibrational place at all times. You can be on a deeply healing journey and you will still get angry. You will still overreact. This has been one of the hardest lessons for me. There is no greater feeling than the love of the Holy Spirit flowing through your body; you're happy, smiling at strangers, eager to help people, all the good things, right? But we must make peace with the dark, heavy feelings that also come up. This doesn't mean that you're not doing the work, or working hard enough; it simply means you are human. And on those days when you're feeling off, it's not an indication of losing any ground. You are always moving forward, even when it doesn't feel like it. So let this be an invitation to you, my friend, to let yourself off the hook and grant yourself some grace. You are doing beautiful, healing work.

So what do we do if we start noticing people in our world who don't vibe with us anymore? As mentioned, this is inevitable; you will lose people, some you love deeply. This is all part of the journey – as you come into greater alignment with yourself, those people and situations that are not in that same alignment must fall away. You will grieve. You will grow. You will expand to even greater levels of yourself. This is what you came here to do. This is what your soul has been leading you towards. I lost some of the most cherished, respected people in my world because their vibration didn't match mine anymore. This was not the way I would have chosen for the situations to occur, but when you commit to Spirit and ask for your guides to intervene, you have to trust that the guidance is for your best. And while I did grieve the loss of these people, my life opened up in extraordinary, incredible ways as soon as the attachments were severed. Severe pain in my body lessened, more money started coming in, and magical opportunities leading me towards my goals appeared. I began showing up with more confidence, more courage, more of who I am supposed to be in this life. It is an extraordinary act of courage to trust that God has your back through all of this, even when it makes no sense, or hurts like hell. Keep going. Keep asking for guidance. Keep trusting. You've got this!

Sometimes you will pick up some toxic energy from a loved one who is supposed to remain in your life. What do we do when this happens? I have a very dear soul sister/friend who lives overseas. Her name is Danique. We met as a result of Breast Implant Illness, and we created a beautiful friendship that was born out of our pain and our journey to loving ourselves deeper. One evening, after a particularly emotional conversation, I offered to send her Reiki. The beautiful thing about Reiki is that it can be sent over any distance and be just as powerful as if the person were in the same room with you.

Danique gratefully accepted my offer, so before I went to sleep I slipped into the energy of healing for her. Reiki is channeled through the body so it's not something that is going to deplete my energy. The energy comes from Source; I am just the vessel it travels.

I channeled for about twenty minutes or so, then fell into a beautiful sleep. But when I woke in the morning, my body was in so much pain, I could hardly move. I felt like I was going to die. I spent most of the day in bed trying to figure out why I felt so crappy, never imagining that it was related to my experience from the night before. Whenever I do this work on clients, I have rituals and prayers that I use to protect my energy from anything that may be influenced by theirs. It didn't occur to me to protect my energy with Danique because I consider her my family. Not only do I love her dearly, but she is also a very mindful, conscious, high-vibrational being doing her soul's work. I trust her. I trust her energy. I never even considered I would need protection from anything she had going on. I was wrong. Being the painfully stubborn human I am, it was well into day two of feeling like absolute shit before I finally realized what was going on. I went into the bathroom to release my bowels and was surprised when the smell of toxins filled the air. Breast implants are filled with heavy metals and the scent of them leaving my body was burning the inside of my nose! As my implants had been removed two years earlier, before I even met Danique, I knew that I was pulling *her* toxins through my body!

This was a real eye-opener for me. Even though I'd been doing this work for many years, I didn't realize I could pull this pain and the actual toxins through my energy field during a healing session. This experience showed me just how powerful we are as energetic beings and that in order to live our best lives, we must protect our energy, even with people we love and hold dear. We can love them and support them, and even share healing with them, but it's not our responsibility to take their pain, just as it's not their responsibility to take on ours. We are all each responsible for our own energy and healing. So how do we go about living a high-vibrational life, and sift through all the toxicity that does not belong to us, without alienating all the people we love? There are rituals and prayers for protection that you can start doing to help you on your path. I've listed some of my favorites below.

Cleansing Rituals

Sage: This can be used as needed to clear any space, including your house, car, office, and even your surrounding energy body. Light the tip of the wand, then blow gently on the flame to extinguish it and produce the smoke. The sage can be held up and away from your body as you move throughout any open space, or held near as you move the stick from your crown to your feet, allowing the smoke to swirl around your entire body. As you allow the smoke to permeate your energetic space, you can say to yourself or out loud any intentions you'd like to set forth. I always like to start with statements of gratitude, such as, "Thank you for clearing away any negative, toxic energies that may have attached to any area within or around my body." Then I speak on what I'd like to bring into my body. "As these attachments leave my body, please replace them with white light, love, joy, peace, happiness, contentment," et cetera. This is where you get to create the rituals that feel the best for you. Whatever you want to call in is what is needed. Sometimes I call in the courage and confidence to make brave decisions and bold moves in my life. You might choose something else. These are your sacred practices so it's totally up to you. Make them a beautiful reflection of your deepest desires. As you move through your intentions, breathe deeply, putting your attention on breathing in that which you are calling forth. Your breath will help move the negative energy out and pull in the feelings you want to feel. You will begin to feel it inside your body. This is how you know when you're complete.

Palo Santo: This can be used just as you used the sage. One of my favorite ways to embody the magic of this holy wood, as well as with sage, is to dance slowly and rhythmically with the smoke, letting it swirl up and around the movement of my body. Moving the body is a great way to shake off any energetic bugs that may be hanging on, especially through the belly and hips. Listen to your body. It will tell you if it needs slow and rhythmic or crazy, booty-shaking moves. Honor whatever She chooses.

Epsom Salt Bath: This is a great way to clear the energetic body as well as soothe physical aches and pains. Create a mood for yourself with candles, music; lock the door if necessary. You can even add essential oils to the water for extra support. Be mindful of the measurement you add, as it is straight magnesium and can affect your bowels if too much is used. A hot bath is also a great space to close your eyes and call forth intentions you'd like to set into motion and/or work with affirmations. Feel into the hot water, breathe in slow and deep, and affirm, "I am at peace. I am free. I am cleansed from the energy of my day." Again, make these your own. Whatever speaks to you is exactly what your spirit is calling for. There's no way to get this wrong.

Hot Shower: You'd be surprised by how this simple act can cleanse, uplift, and inspire all at once. I personally receive such great intuitive downloads in the shower. There's something magical about it that I cannot explain. I have many friends and colleagues who also talk of abundant spiritual input and clarity while in the shower. They tell me they receive their best ideas here. Give it a try! See if it doesn't start working some magic in your world as well.

Imagery Using White or Golden Light: This is excellent for protection as well as cleansing and clearing. Envision yourself surrounded by this light; you can also envision a shower of white or golden light as an alternative to an actual shower. Remember, anything you can envision, and draw the energy of, through your body, you can create. Your power lies in your intention; it is all you really need to begin working with Spirit, at any time, wherever you may be.

Prayers for Protection

These can be as simple as you need them to be. Don't over-think your words. Spirit knows your heart and hears you even if you are still trying to figure out what words feel the best for you. The following are some that I've used and tweaked over the last twenty years. Feel free to make them your own.

"Father God, Holy Mother, Beloved angels, ancestors, and guides, thank you for protecting me today from anything that is not in alignment with my highest good."

"Thank you, spirit team, for protecting me to and from all of my destinations today." (Anytime I enter my car.)

"Archangel Michael, please protect me today from any negative energies or entities, seen or unseen, that may cross my path."

These are just a sprinkling of ways to cleanse and protect your beautiful energetic self. As you go deeper into your work, your guides will lead you to that which is best for you. You are being taught to trust the way Spirit shows up for you. This in turn teaches you how to trust the guidance you receive and, ultimately, trust yourself. You are the authority in your own life. Spirit is just here to remind you of that. You have the power at all times to choose what's best for you.

THE ESSENCE OF FAE

In the simplest of terms, the essence of Fae is joy – pure, outrageous, unapologetic joy. I believe we are born into this world as channels of that joy. It is our birthright, and we own within ourselves the capacity to be and feel it. It is this joy that ignites our being and body to create the magic that is our life. The energy of delight is what allows you to tune in to your body's vibrational pull and create the things your heart desires. This is what I meant in the introduction when I spoke of using your body as a magic wand.

We are quantum beings held gently in the universal embrace of vibration and frequency. This means that you truly have the power to create anything you desire in this life by simply raising your frequency to align with those experiences you are drawn to. So why aren't we enjoying ourselves more then? Let's explore that question and dive into some ways we can reclaim joy in our lives.

Take a walk with me, friend, back to a time when you were a young child. Take my hand, you are safe here. Look around, as we walk through your neighborhood. Your eyes are bright, wide, taking in all the colors, the shapes, the smells of nature's beauty wafting across your face. You're turning this way and that; you just can't seem to get enough. You stop at a rose bush and bury your face into a bright pink bloom. I hear you inhale deeply. You turn to me, smiling ear to ear. This is joy. We walk along further. A cool breeze whispers across our cheeks. You giggle. I can't help but smile watching you. You take off running ahead about twenty-five feet. You stop, turn to face the sky, and with arms outstretched, you begin to twirl. I catch up to you, turn to face the sky, and with arms outstretched, I begin to twirl as well. This is joy. You grab my hand and lead me further down the sidewalk. I am looking off to the side at the wise, old oaks that line the street when I hear you gasp. I look over to see an enormous black and yellow butterfly dancing around your face. Your eyes are lit up, watching it dart back and forth. I watch it land on your nose. You freeze. You just made a friend. It looks you in the eye, gives you a gentle kiss and flies off. This is joy. The energy of nature, the essence of Fae are one and the same.

Do you remember ever having an experience like this as a child, an experience with a trusted adult where you were given freedom to explore your world and be curious about everything that crossed your path? I don't. Don't get me wrong, I was exposed to many different opportunities to explore my world, but they each were tainted with the negative thoughts, beliefs and fears of whoever was in charge of my care in that moment. This meant that I could experience my world only to the degree of their limitations, which wasn't much at all.

I remember a time when I was about nine years old. I had been out and about in the neighborhood for most of the afternoon. On my way back home, I passed by a beautiful oleander bush that towered over me. It was filled with white blooms.

My precious heart leapt at the opportunity to pick some of the flowers to take home to my mom. I gathered a small bouquet and with a smile on my face, proudly walked home. I bounced in the front door and ran up to her, holding out the flowers.

"Mom!" I exclaimed, "Look what I brought for you!"

Instead of the delight I was expecting, a look of horror flashed across her face and she slapped the bouquet out of my hands.

"Those are poisonous! Don't ever touch those!"

I stood there and watched while she dumped the flowers into the garbage can. I don't remember what happened after that, but a wound was created that day. It took me many years to come to an understanding of what had happened and why. But that is just one example of how we are taught to forget our joy. Does this stir any memories for you? Can you think of a time when a well-meaning parent or other adult projected their fear onto you and altered the way you see and experience your world? These experiences are so potent and profound and yet we easily dismiss them as nothing. As adults it's easy to do. And even though children bounce back quickly because they live to please their loved ones, the body keeps track of each time someone stole a piece of joy from them. And because the body keeps track, it also is in charge of when the healing to release the wound will occur.

As you read through this book, don't be surprised if memories begin to surface and wounds begin to open up. This book is a healing journey for you. It's a healing journey for me too! This is why it's taken over ten years to bring it to life. The wounds we sustain as children run deep. But the love of Spirit runs deeper. This is your time. Your body is ready to release the wounds that have stifled your joy. Now let's dive into some ways to get that back!

Pleasure

We are born as creative vessels built for pleasure. Pleasure lives and breathes within our senses, permeating each cell with divine love. We arrive knowing that our bodies are living, breathing miracles capable of bringing life into the world. And, like joy, pleasure is our birthright. There are unlimited ways to experience the delights of this life. The trick is to get out of our own way while doing it. When I think of pleasure, I immediately think of making love or self-pleasure. This is a beautiful way to reconnect yourself to your inner joy. If you are in partnership with someone, ideally you both love and respect each other and have created a safe, intimate space to explore each other sexually. Because we are human, intimate relationships will always open up to deeper levels of healing between lovers. Triggers that arise during lovemaking are not necessarily cause for alarm, but an opportunity for communication, compassion, and understanding. Of course, there are many complex layers to this, so please be sure you're in a healthy union before exploring this further. If you're not completely comfortable with your partner, do not force the issue. Instead, see it as an opportunity for you to go deeper within yourself to better understand what needs to change in the relationship. But only you know that which you need to feel safe in this situation.

Let's journey into the space of pleasure with your partner. Engage all your senses. This is a time for feeling into the experience, not focusing on the end result of orgasm, yours or theirs. Gaze into each other's eyes, release attachment to what you think you look like and get into your body and how it feels to be caressed and held. Are there areas you love to be touched? Invite your partner in to enjoy those areas with you. Let him or her kiss you there, lick you there, surrendering to the sensation, allowing your body to feel. You may even be surprised to discover places you never even considered erogenous, such as the back of your elbow or the tiny caverns that live in your clavicle. Most of us have been raised to shut down our feelings, and our bodies are so armored with trauma, which means that safe, sensual touch can be a wonderful gateway to healing.

In this space you are being invited to surrender fully to the feelings that arise. Let yourself speak out your pleasure. Your voice is safe here, so give Her permission to be heard. Let Her moan or groan; she may even need to growl or snort. Let Her. She's safe. Her sexual expression is safe. Your feeling of complete comfort in your skin and allowing your partner to witness it will create even more arousal, making the experience vibrate even higher into the ethers. Yes, sacred sex raises a person's vibration, and raising your own automatically raises the vibration of the planet. That is the goal here.

Now don't go thinking you need to be in partnership with someone in order for this to work for you. You don't. It has been many, many moons since I've had a partner in my life to explore this with. And while it feels great to have someone special in your life, the most important relationship you will ever have is the one you create with yourself. My time alone has been some of the best and greatest therapy I could ever wish for. Yours can be too! This is a time for exploring your body in all Her glory; what She likes, what She doesn't. What are you willing to try? What hang-ups do you need to let go of? Are you open to receive? This is important. Most of us struggle with receiving. We can give, give, give, but when it comes to receiving, we shut down for myriad reasons. As you begin to explore yourself, those reasons are bound to pop up. Send them love, thank them for their service, and give them permission to leave. You no longer need them. Keeping a journal during your self-exploration is a valuable tool to keep track of the things that emerge. I know when I first began exploring myself, I couldn't get past the deep shame I would feel. Shame is one of those emotions that runs deep. It travels between generations and lives in our DNA, which means that it may not even be your shame that you feel. It could belong to your mother, grandmother, or back even further in your female lineage. It requires immense patience, presence, and love in order to move it out of the body. I know, because it took me years. If shame is a big one for you, be gentle with yourself as you move through it. Whatever emotion arises, keep sending it love, keep sending yourself love. It will move, I promise you.

This time of self-discovery may also trigger repressed memories of abuse in either this life or past lifetimes. If this happens, do not panic. Depending on the nature and intensity of the memories, you may want to seek out professional help to assist you in making sense of the experience. And while traditional therapy is helpful, you may also benefit from regular bodywork sessions and somatic work. The wounds of abuse live in your cells and, unfortunately, they cannot be talked out. They must be moved out physically. If you feel secure in yourself to sit with your own pain and allow it to move through, then this will be a very potent, powerful time of expansion and healing for you. We will explore in a later chapter practices and techniques to help you move physical and emotional pain out of your body. This is a process of remembering who you are, of reclaiming your power and remembering that you are worthy of a magical and fulfilling life. Taking control of your own pleasure is one of the best gifts you can ever give yourself.

There truly are no limits to how you choose to reclaim pleasure for yourself. The joy you are seeking can be found in anything that requires you to engage your senses. The idea here is to take yourself out of your mind where overthinking and fear can intrude, putting a stop to your joy. This is how you get out of your own way. So, let's look at some other ways to bring back pleasure into our lives.

- **Embrace the Joy of Food**: This includes food-growing, preparing, tasting, throwing dinner parties, taking cooking classes, and so many other ways.

- **Gardening**: This has been one of the most profound healing techniques for me. There is something incredibly powerful about putting your hands directly into the earth and nurturing a form of life that brings value to the entire planet. Plus, it's a great way to connect with the faery realm if you're just starting out. The Fae love to help those who help the Earth!

- **Singing:** This is a powerful way to raise your vibration and have a ton of fun while doing it. It doesn't matter if you think you're a good singer or not – the freeing of your voice is what counts! Choose songs that light up your soul when you hear them. Don't let your inner critic have a say. She's not welcome at this show!

- **Dancing:** This is another powerful way to have fun and bring back joy into your life. And like the singing, it does not matter what you think you look like while doing it. Just get that body moving! Choose your favorite songs and set yourself free. You're going to feel so great; you're not even going to be paying attention to anything or anyone else.

What other ways can you think of to bring joy back into your life? Is there a hobby of yours that got put on the back burner? Is there something new you've been wanting to try? This is the time! Those ideas and inspiration are Spirit trying to get your attention, to bring you back to that place of delight in your world.

Take my hand again friend. We're going out to play! Yes, I said play. I am inviting you back to a time when living life was effortless and filled with delight. A time when the only thing you needed to worry about was the sun going down for the day. Play has been one of the most surprising ways that I've learned to connect with the faery realm, and connect more deeply with myself.

In the early days of my work with Fae, I found that swinging in the park was the easiest and quickest way to connect to their energy. This was one of my favorite things to do outside when I was a child. I felt light, free, as if I was one with the air. The moment my feet left the ground, a silly smile would spread wide across my face. I couldn't control it. I did not want to. This too, is pure, outrageous joy. At first, I just soaked in the feelings of euphoria, not able to make sense of any of it. It started with the hairs on my neck standing on end. Then the goosebumps would begin working their way down my body. Now I've experienced goosebumps before, but never across my cheeks and nose. I had tapped into something magical, that's for sure. I began to look for any way I could to tap into this feeling. I learned that simply setting the intention to connect was all that was necessary for the Fae to swoop in and delight me with their wisdom. As with any spirit guide or angel, all you have to do is ask for their assistance and they are happy to help. Each time I went to the park or called in the Fae, I was gifted more guidance, more wisdom. It came in the form of ideas, thoughts, and creative inspiration. I would wake up and feel an immediate need to go to the park. This urge was them calling me, tuning into the frequency that my body was already attuned to. I've come to know that the Universe knows our deepest soul desires, even when we aren't aware of them, and because of this, knows exactly what to do to inspire you to a place of connection. My faery guides introduced me to the swings over and over again, bringing me closer and closer to the heart of their message. If you are willing to let your guard down and let your inner child out to play, you will most certainly be gifted with the energy of delight straight from the faery realm. They are masters of play! Here are a few more of my favorite ways to connect with my inner fae.

- **Blow bubbles:** as many and as often as possible! Much like the swings, bubbles have special magic that lights people up instantly. One of the best places to keep bubbles in case of an emergency is in your car. Think of all the times you're stuck in traffic, tired, maybe a little grumpy, bust out with some bubbles and lighten up your ride. It works every time! Also, if possible, keeping some handy in your office is a great way to bring some joy to your workday. In my previous jobs I never had my own office, so I would just go out by my car on my lunch break and blow them outside. I liked this better because it got me outdoors.

- **Mud pies:** Yep, I said it. Get outside and whip yourself up some mud pies! When my sister and I were kids, we loved doing this with our cousins. It's a cold, messy, sensory extravaganza. Give it a try, you'll love it! And if you really want to have some fun with it, take your freshly made pies and vigorously throw them at the side of your house or a surrounding wall outside and see how many stick. This was a game we played as kids. We got into trouble every single time, but I'll never forget the fun we had doing it. And since you are the grown-up in your house, you make the rules. Nobody is going to tell you no or yell at you for making a mess that can easily be sprayed off with the hose.

- **Sprinklers:** Run through them every chance you get! (Well, provided the weather isn't uncomfortably cold.) There's something about the spray of chilly water spattering your face to make a person come alive with joy. I am a former marathon runner, and when I was running on a regular basis I loved passing by a yard or park with sprinklers on. I never missed an opportunity to run through them. Not only did it cool me off, but it brought my inner Erin out, squealing with delight. You can't help but giggle when you run through them. I truly believe our memories from childhood get reactivated when we give ourselves permission to play. This is such a healthy outlet for us as adults. We work too much and take life way too seriously. We must give ourselves permission to play; our lives truly depend on it.

- **Skipping:** I believe all adults would benefit greatly from adding skipping into their daily routine. Headed to your car, skip! Going out to check the mailbox, skip! Taking the dog for a walk, skip! Wherever ye may walk, skip! Try it. I dare you! Once your legs lift the ground, your arms start swinging and the next thing you know you're propelling yourself down the sidewalk and giggling like a fool because you've got pure outrageous joy surging through your veins.

Now I realize that the thought of doing any of these activities might trigger some fear and discomfort. We fear looking foolish. We fear feeling awkward. We might get laughed at. People might point and stare. As I write this, I'm reminded of an episode of *Friends* when Rachel joins Phoebe running in the park. Rachel is totally embarrassed running beside Phoebe because her arms flail about while her legs awkwardly gallop down the sidewalk. Phoebe could not care less. She's a free spirit and completely at ease in her body and the way it runs. She's having fun and she knows it. Her joy is what's important, not what others may think. Rachel is mortified. Moral of the story? Be Phoebe. If we desire to create more joy and fun in our life, we must be willing to release attachment to other people's thoughts and opinions of us. It's one of the greatest ways we hold ourselves back from the life we say we want.

It's possible there's a deeper reason you fear trying these activities. Let's say there was a day when you were about five years old, and you were leaving the grocery store with your mom. She was pushing the basket and instead of walking beside her, you took off skipping across the parking lot without even looking and almost got hit by a car. She started screaming and running towards you, but instead of hugging you close and checking to see that you're safe, she unleashes an angry tirade about how stupid you are for running off and how foolish it was of you to not look for passing cars. As a child, you needed to feel safe in that moment. You looked to your mom for that security and love, but it didn't come. In that moment, a wound was created, so even the thought of skipping may trigger strong emotions in you. You may not even know why initially. If you feel triggered by any of these play options, don't be afraid to explore them deeper. Once you get to the root of your resistance, you will be able to understand why the emotion was triggered and allow it to move out of your experience altogether. This will give you an opportunity to reclaim those things that once brought you great joy and allow for forgiveness to take place between you and whoever played a role in that painful experience.

THE PURPOSE OF PAIN

I knew that this would be a challenging chapter to write, which is probably why it's one of the last to be completed. I feel like most of my adult life has been spent navigating my way through varying degrees of pain, physical and emotional. And while I have created and cultivated a beautiful, magical life, and love the woman I have become, it has come as a result of walking through that pain. I speak on being taken through initiations in another chapter, but these experiences are almost all triggered by pain.

There's not a person on the planet who doesn't experience pain in some form or another. It is my hope that reading this will help you come to an acceptance and understanding of your own pain and give you some ways to help manage and/or release it forever. I am going to ask you to be willing to sit with your pain. I know that's asking a lot, but it is the first step in learning how to let pain be a teacher and guide for you. We have to be willing to accept what is so that we can make room for what may be. I'll be honest – pain sucks. But it's not in vain. It has a purpose and a plan. It is a treasure chest carrying valuable pieces of wisdom for you. If you can be open and willing to look on your pain from this perspective, you are already well on your way to the peace and ease your body and soul so desperately craves.

The human body is a vessel and a channel of the Holy Spirit. And, as you've been learning in this book, the Holy Spirit can move through our experience in many beautiful ways. Because we are a vessel, we have the capacity to hold the entire Universe inside our being. We *are* the entire Universe. It's just that simple. Because of this, however, we also have the capacity to feel and hold that which belongs to others. Sometimes we are aware of this and sometimes not. I've spent the better part of my adult life learning how to hold only my own "stuff" – meaning my own pain, thoughts, feelings, behaviors, patterns, et cetera. I know I came to this planet to help serve the greater good of humanity. In the early days of this awareness, I would do whatever I could to take another's pain away from them because I couldn't bear to see them hurt. Then another person would come along my path, and I'd take their pain too. Before long I'd collected massive amounts of pain that didn't even belong to me. I've always been one of those people that others found easy to talk to. People are always quick to share their stories with me, the deeper the better. If you are one of those people, you are probably walking around with physical and/or emotional pain that isn't even yours.

Take a moment right now, close your eyes, take in a deep breath, and tune in to your body. Start at the top of your head and scan yourself down to your toes. Notice any areas of pain. What does it feel like? When you put your attention on it, what's the first thing that comes to mind? Is it something tangible like a person or experience, or maybe a conversation you had, perhaps an emotion that pops up? Can you identify the emotion? Think about how long you've had the pain in your body. Scanning your body like this is one of the easiest ways to begin healing your pain. Let your curiosity lead you. Ask questions, and trust your body to tell you the truth. Even if it doesn't make sense or feels awkward, trust yourself. As you get more comfortable connecting with your pain, you will be able to discern whether it is yours or someone else's. If it does belong to someone else, you then have the opportunity to learn from it and release it back to the Universe to be transmuted into light. If the pain is yours, continue being curious, asking questions, so that you can clarify what it is here to teach you. Once its lesson has been learned, it too will go.

Pain is really just a way to draw you closer to the source power you were born from. God, the Holy Spirit, your higher self, the Universe, whatever you resonate with – it's all the same loving energy that wants you to feel loved and at peace in your body and in your world. My deepest pain has brought me so close to God that I weep in gratitude when I think about it. I remember a time in 2014 when a tooth in the back of my mouth was in need of a root canal. Because of the process and possibility of infection, I was not willing to get that done. I decided to have it pulled out instead. It was the last tooth on the top right side, so I wasn't worried about missing it.

If you've ever experienced tooth pain, you know how excruciating it can be. While I waited for my appointment, I was prescribed Vicodin for the pain. I do not like putting anything pharmaceutical into my body if I can help it. I was terrified of becoming dependent upon it. I was using clove oil, but it just wasn't helping. I broke down one night and took a dose of the Vicodin. It did not help my pain one bit! I was beside myself. I couldn't see straight, I couldn't think straight, I thought I was going to lose my mind. I remember standing in my kitchen sobbing, holding the bottle of pills in one hand, thinking that maybe if I took a whole bunch then I wouldn't be in pain anymore. I didn't care about any consequences; I just couldn't bear the pain any longer. I stood there staring at the pills for the longest time. I was alone. I felt as if there was no one I could reach out to. Suddenly I felt this gentle but insistent urge to go outside. It was after midnight and I didn't really want to, but the feeling wouldn't let up. At the time, I lived in a very small, courtyard complex that I felt very safe walking in even late at night, so finally I surrendered and stepped outside. I started walking down the sidewalk, and as I neared the bend, I saw my neighbor Sarah sitting out on her porch having a drink. I don't remember what she said, I don't remember what I said, but within ninety seconds of connecting with her, I was able to return to my apartment. I will never forget that night. I wanted to end my life. The pain was too much to bear. God was calling me, knowing that all I needed was to step outside, breathe in the fresh air, and follow the gentle guidance down to Sarah's house. That night I was able to sleep well for the first time in weeks.

Pain can also be an indicator of something that is out of alignment within yourself. Let's say that you talk constantly about your dream job or a goal that's been on your heart to achieve your whole life. You talk and talk and talk about it. It holds a big space inside you, waiting, waiting, waiting, for you to take a step in that direction. Your spirit is waiting for you to take action. Speaking on your dreams is great, but if you don't take action, your words fall flat. When this happens, the body may step in and bring some pain into your life. Let's go back to your dream job. While you speak about this job and let your mind wonder about it day in and day out, you are working at a job that sucks the life out of you and makes you dread getting up each day. You may begin to feel that dread in the pit of your stomach. It may be a fleeting sensation every once in a while, but you suddenly notice it's showing up daily now. Its intensity is growing and instead of it being a quick one-and-done, it's now staying with you all day, and at times has you doubled over. If you begin to notice unexplained pain showing up in your body, before you run off to the doctor and drop a bunch of money on tests and pills, take some time to get to know your pain. Start looking for patterns in its presentation. What time of day does it begin? Is it every day? How long does it last? Does it only show up in certain situations? It could even be something in your diet that needs to change. These are all things you can become clear on just by embracing your pain and letting your curiosity lead the way.

I've struggled my entire adult life with lower back pain. I have always been very active and healthy, though, so it wouldn't affect me too badly. But over the last several years, the pain had increased in intensity and duration. Some days I couldn't even get out of bed. I couldn't walk, I couldn't sit or stand, I could only lay down propped up with pillows. It got to the point where I couldn't even exercise anymore. Now, as mentioned, my pain journey is unique in that my purpose in this life is to process pain through my body for my own evolution as well as the collective consciousness. I am here on assignment to transmute pain into purpose and light and to teach others how to do the same. What this means is that I feel pain in my body a lot! But I know that when this happens, I have the tools to move it through. I've learned to accept my pain, sit quietly with it, and learn from it. There is so much we can learn from our pain and the pain experienced by others. Ultimately, my excessive low back pain was a result of working a job that took very good care of me and my family financially but was not in alignment with my soul. I had expanded my vibration so greatly that I was no longer able to withstand the lower vibration of the working environment I was in. I ended up quitting so that I could put my full energy and attention into what my soul was calling me to do. Now I very rarely have back pain, and when I do I know that it's either not mine, or Spirit is calling me to do something. Either way, I am able to release it easily once the clarity has been accessed inside my being.

What are some other reasons pain might show up in your body? This is where it can get fun – and you can learn some fascinating things about yourself – if you are willing to let your inner scientist out to play. The body will let you know if it's time to change something in your diet, either by removing items or adding something in. Your body will let you know if you need more exercise, more rest, even more play! Yes, it's true! If you are working too much and taking life way too seriously, your body could manifest pain to alert you that you need some fun. This is where you have to be willing to let your curiosity lead the way. As a collective, we are so quick to run off to the doctor for answers and drugs, when our beautiful bodies will tell us everything we need to know. Now, I'm not saying to never go to the doctor because of course that is a necessary and valuable part of being human and western medicine absolutely has its place in our life. However, I am inviting you to give yourself an opportunity to know your body more intimately. It carries an intelligence far greater than any doctor's prescription. It builds trust in yourself and allows you to fully embrace your sovereignty as a spirit being living in a human body.

Pain is power. Do you believe that? Do you feel anything in your body when you read those words? It feels pretty nervy of me to make that statement. When pain invades our body, we have a choice. We can either choose to embrace it, use it as fuel to propel us forward, and learn everything we can from it, or we can succumb to its gnarly grasp and let it consume us. For years I let my back pain and all the other unexplained pains control my life. My pain became my story, and my story became me. Has this ever happened to you? Every day I lived with pain, I spoke about my pain, I gave it all my power because – let's face it – it was winning. I hurt. Somedays I could smile through the pain, but many days all I could do was cry. I didn't like it, I didn't want it, and I felt powerless to change it. But the more I began working with my faery guides, my story started to change. I learned that I do have a choice.

We are not our pain. We are not our story. We are vibrational beings capable of anything we put our attention on. It's in our DNA. We have all the power. We need only flip the switch on our narrative to begin to see a new way. Your pain is not your enemy; your thoughts and feelings towards your pain is your enemy. But you, my friend, have always had the power to transform any part of your experience you are not in alignment with. Yes, I will say it again. You are that powerful! What story are you telling yourself right now? Is it a story of triumph and grace? Or is it a story of pain keeping you stuck in the woe-is-me of your life? What story would you love to start living right now? Begin it. Make the choice to use your pain as power and let it burn through everything that you are not so that you may emerge all that you are. You are a worthy, beautiful, inspiring light of God! Do not for one more minute let your pain try to tell you otherwise.

We've spent quite a bit of time delving into physical pain and the ways it can show up in the body. But what about emotional pain? Unexpressed emotional pain can also manifest as low back pain or any other physical pain you may feel. But it can also manifest as depression, anxiety, eating disorders, addictions, overworking, and OCD, to name a few. My low back is my main pain hub, so whether it's physical pain or emotional it's more than likely to move through that area. Emotional pain can also show up as shifts and distortions on the body such as lumps, bumps, curves, and bends.

Think about your feet for a moment. How do you feel about your feet? Is it safe to say you don't like them? Have you ever wondered why? Our emotional trauma and the stories attached to it can be stored in the body and show up as physical distortions in the feet and toes. When I was going through my massage therapy program I decided to specialize in Reflexology and Toe Reading, a fascinating area of study that I had never experienced before. The feet and toes represent our path, where we've come from, and where we're going. The feet hold our stories and the secrets surrounding our pain. We have the power to change the shape of our feet and toes simply by changing our thoughts and healing the emotions that are living inside our bodies. This has become some of my greatest work with clients because it is so incredibly potent. The following is my personal testimony to the power of this work, and why I am so passionate about what I do.

I'm going to get really vulnerable here for a minute. I want to illustrate the power of the feet and their ability to hold on to the pain of our traumas and the miracle of transformation and healing that takes place when someone creates a safe space for us to be heard. In January of 2018 I called a friend I've known for several years for a ride home from a pub. My usual two glasses of wine were hitting me harder than normal, and it felt safer than calling an Uber. It wasn't. He raped me.

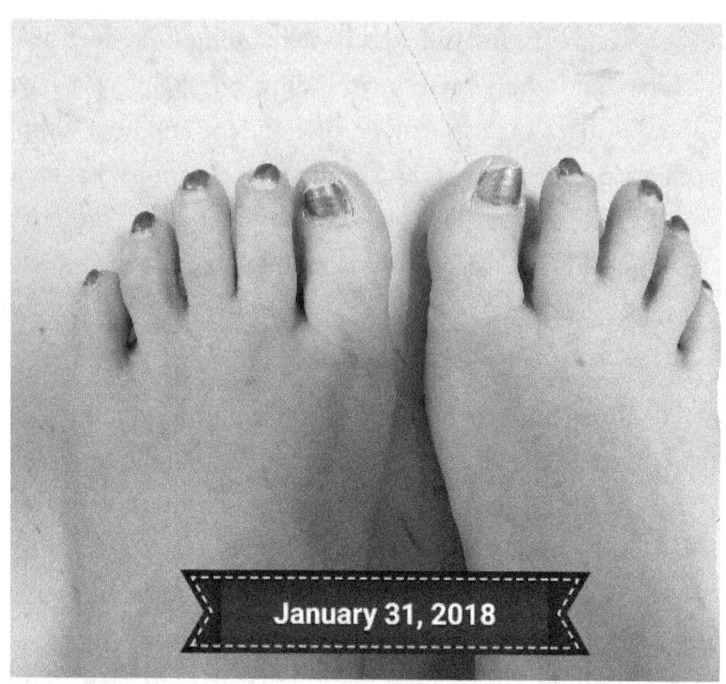

January 31, 2018

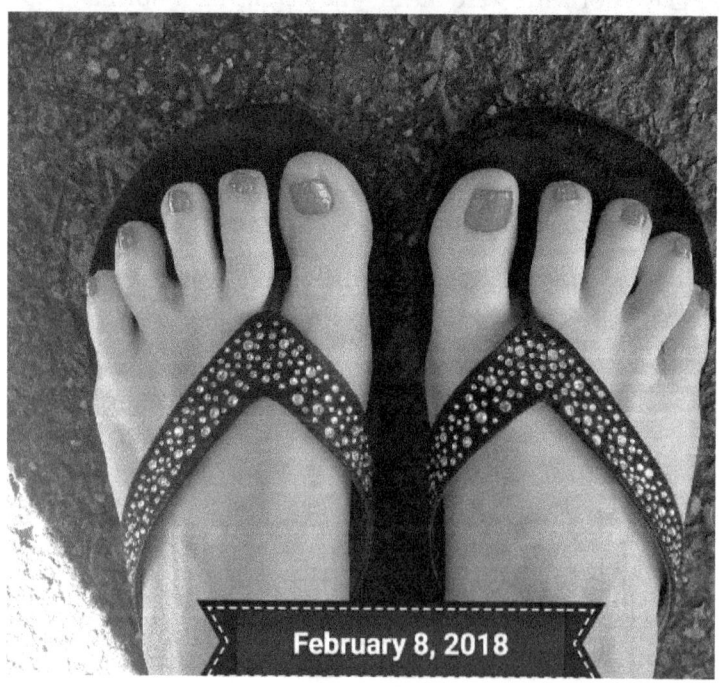

February 8, 2018

The top picture are my toes three days after that incident. They were inflamed, hot to the touch, they literally looked like they were boiling with rage, seething. Most of the toes are not even touching the ground. This is a woman who desperately wants off this earth. When being in the body feels too painful, the toes will literally lift off the ground, a physical manifestation of a spirit trying to leave the body. There are only eight days between the pictures. It was during those eight days that I attended several reflexology classes. During one class in particular (auriculotherapy, or reflexology of the ear), I was asked to share my experience about something completely unrelated to this and I just kept saying how angry I felt but couldn't understand why. My teacher/mentor Cheryl came over to me and, somewhat like a playground bully, she began poking me in the shoulder, egging me on. "Come on Erin, you want to hit me?" Now, Cheryl and I had developed a beautiful, supportive rapport over the course of my program so I knew I could trust her fully; I also knew she holds mad, magical space for healing, so even though I had no idea what she was up to I just stood there, letting her get under my skin. She grabbed a bolster pillow, held it to her midsection, and kept bullying me, and the next thing I knew I was up out of my chair punching her with everything I've got. Then I was kicking at her and screaming – all with a classroom of students looking on.

At that moment I left my body and was watching in awe at the situation unfolding around me. I felt so much love and support, and was suddenly aware that I absolutely did not want to hurt this beautiful soul standing strong in my corner. I turned away from Cheryl and with my bare feet started kicking the wall. This experience lasted maybe five minutes, I don't know, but the bottom picture speaks for itself. This is the very nature of toe reading.

Put simply, our toes hold the stories and traumas of our life. If I hadn't been given the safety and support to move this experience out of my body, that trauma would start to grow. It would infiltrate my cells, my organs, my entire being. Something like this left unattended has the capacity to birth cancer in a person. This is the healing power of the human body. This is the power you hold inside of you, every minute of every day. Yes, YOU are that powerful! Not all shifts are this extreme, but they are all equally profound and powerful. A simple change in thinking has the power to move your life in a completely different direction. All it takes is one question to get you wondering, remembering, curious about that one thing you thought was over. The body remembers. When it is time to look at it again, nothing can stop the energy from moving. Your spirit longs for peace and freedom. You are always on the path towards that. Trust yourself. Trust your body. Trust your feet. They are not ugly or deformed, they are showing you something that is ready to heal. Give them grace. Love them as much as you can. After all, they carry you through each day.

I still get emotional when I tell this story. In order for me to do the work that I do and be able to hold space for women to heal their own traumas, I had to be willing to look deeply into my own pain. I had to pay attention to what was happening on the inside of me as well as the outside. This showing up in my feet was a direct reflection of all the anger, rage, and fear that I felt that night when I was too afraid to tell this man no. I was too afraid to stand up for myself because I feared for my safety. Because of my history of sexual abuse, it felt safer to just surrender knowing that at least I'd walk away alive. But this experience has changed me. The boiling anger and rage that erupted out of me has become my power. I am no longer willing to stand down in the face of abuse. My voice is strong now and I'm not afraid to use it. This experience taught me how to reclaim my power and gather back those pieces of my soul that had been shattered from years of abuse. Interestingly enough, as soon as I reclaimed this part of myself, I stopped attracting men who disrespected and abused me. They either quit coming around or I courageously told them where they could go. I've never felt stronger and more liberated as a woman than I do right now. I wouldn't wish this experience on anyone, but I love the woman I've become because of it. This is one of the great purposes of pain. We can use it to birth ourselves into the real-life superheroes that this world needs. This world desperately needs strong voices, fearless leaders, and courageous visionaries willing to see the darkness through a new lens of possibility and light. The fact that you're reading this book shows me that you too are one of the called to help bring this planet to a new light. We are the ones this world has been waiting on!

Working with my guides and learning how to honor and listen to my body has shown me some of the most magical aspects of life that continue to blow my mind. One of my most vivid experiences occurred in 2020, during a time when my back seemed to be going out every week. The pain was ridiculous and I had no idea what to do about it, except surrender. Every time my back would flare up, it felt as if I was in labor again. I labored fourteen hours with no medication to bring my daughter into this world, I know this pain well!

The pain would expand across my low back and wrap completely around my pelvis, then stab its way down my lumbar spine and into the space deep under my belly. I woke up one Monday morning after having a very clear, vivid dream that would plague my mind all day. In the dream I saw myself looking down between my legs. I noticed something sticking out of my vagina. Curious, I reached down and pulled gently on it. At first it looked like the end of a frazzled rope. But I soon realized it was much larger than a small piece of rope. I pulled and pulled and pulled. At this point I was using both my hands to grab on because the girth was enormous. I pulled on it for what seemed forever and when I finally got to the end, I had pulled out a good four feet of thick, cord-like material. The dream ended there. Two days later I had the same exact dream. And again, when it was over, I had pulled out another four feet or so of thick cord. The cords reminded me of the ties used to hold back heavy, Victorian drapes, but instead of golden, ornate tassels, they were tattered, dirty, old and very heavy. I knew Spirit was trying to tell me something because this was too incredible to just be a passing dream. Now mind you, my back had been out for the three-day span when the dreams occurred.

The dream was heavy on my mind as I stepped gently into the shower that morning. My back would always spasm unexpectedly, bringing me to my knees, and I always found the shower a perfect place to get some light stretching in. The hot water would allow me to move easily into a forward fold yoga position, helping to ease some of the pain and pressure in my back. And, as mentioned earlier, the shower has always been a magical place of connection for me. It's like the water allows Spirit to connect directly and wash off my human distractions so I'm able to hear everything very clearly. As I slowly leaned forward to bend towards the shower floor, I felt my entire womb space open up, allowing me to fold deeper than I ever had before, and with absolutely no pain in my body! I started to cry, feeling the freedom and movement in my hips and spine. My entire womb space felt completely empty.

In that moment I heard Spirit say to me, *"You are free, beautiful girl. Every man that has ever hurt you, disrespected you, stolen a piece of your innocence, every single one has been removed from your womb space. The energy of their transgression is gone. All of it, gone! You are free! You pulled out the cords attached to each experience you endured. You did that. You stood up for yourself once and for all and said no more! Your body, mind, and spirit were all in alignment for your healing. You are a powerful healer, dear child. We want you to remember this from this day forward. Your pain is never in vain. There is always a divine purpose. You always have a choice in how you want to respond to the pain in your body. You chose to empower yourself. This is your moment, your celebration. We applaud you!"*

I stood there bent over in the shower sobbing, touching my belly, my pelvis, feeling the space that was now able to move freely. I had never in my life been able to move this way before! Oh, and that pain that had been surging through my body the last few days…it had completely vanished.

Every pain we experience, whether physical or emotional, has a story to tell. It is up to us as powerful, intuitive beings to tap in, breathe into our fear, release attachment, and find out once and for all what our body is trying to tell us.

BUG LOVE

Since my awakening in 2002, I've had so many incredible, unbelievable experiences with nature. Just when I think I've seen everything, something new presents and shows me once again that this life is a vast, limitless, playground of universal possibility, which is what brings me to this chapter on my adventures with bugs and how to help you see them through new eyes. Not only will you connect deeper in a way to help you coexist more peacefully with the critters and creatures in your world, you will also meet a courageous and empowered, new version of yourself. I will be using the word bug throughout the chapter, even though technically my examples are all insects.

As I began connecting more and more with my faery guides, I discovered a new respect and reverence for the earth. I stepped gently now, lightly, so as not to disturb the life that we typically take for granted. I won't walk on grassy areas unless I absolutely have to. If I happened to be at a park where walking on the grass was unavoidable, I began a practice of announcing myself and asking permission to step into the area. As I got to know my guides, they advised me that I need not ask permission any longer, they always knew when I was coming because they were the ones who called out to me. They informed me that they needed me out in nature as much as possible to learn the ways and the language of the land. So while I no longer ask for permission or tell them I'm going to step into their space, I still move gently with reverence and gratitude. No matter where I go in nature, I can always hear who is calling out to me. Sometimes it's a tree, an open grassy space, a large rock beckoning me to sit with her. Nature speaks in infinite ways and once we understand Her language, we can communicate always.

This is how I began talking with bugs. I began treating them with the same reverence and respect that I did for all my plant guides. This was so much harder to do though in the beginning. Let's be honest, it's still hard at times. I started out slowly by just acknowledging their presence. For example, if something flew into my house, I would welcome it, acknowledge it and let it know that I was going to do my best to get him back outside where he could live his best life. If you're like me, you've been raised with the beliefs that bugs are an annoyance and need to be shooed out or swatted away at all times. And to be clear, there are bugs out there that can harm us. But as I mention later with the bees, learning to be with bugs is about honoring space. We don't have to kill a bug to keep it from harming us. We can find a way to get him back to his home space outside, keeping us both safe.

In 2016 I was living in the smallest space I'd ever inhabited – a six hundred and eighty-four-square-foot apartment with one bedroom and one bathroom. I loved it, though! It was tucked in the corner of a tiny courtyard complex that looked like a real-life faery garden. Every tenant had plants galore on their patios and elemental statues of all kinds. There were fruit trees available for everyone to pick from and everything was so green and alive. I was in love and have never felt more at home than I did there. When I moved in, I made it a point to welcome in any bugs that felt guided to come. I did this with the intention that I would honor them as long as they honored me. Mostly moths visited me, and sometimes these tiny green iridescent faery-looking bugs that I still don't know the name of. But one night I had a visit from a mosquito friend. I was up late writing and noticed him flying around my face. I immediately was triggered. Back then it took an act of God to get me to sit long enough to get any writing done, so whenever I did finally sit down, I did not want to be disturbed, especially by a mosquito. But, remembering the welcome I'd issued when I moved in, I took in a deep breath, said hello, and then proceeded to tell him that I was super busy and really needed him to not be buzzing around me. It was highly distracting, I said, and keeping me from focusing on my work. I was afraid too that he would bite me and that was something I did not want to deal with. I then went on to tell him that I appreciate him paying me a visit and that I had no intention of hurting him at all; I just needed him to leave me be.

I finished my speech, watched him circle my head, and land on the wall to my right about three feet away. I stared at him for the longest time, wondering if he would start moving again. He didn't. I sat at my table for a couple hours and would keep checking over on him, but he never budged, not once.

It was nearing one a.m. and I needed to go to bed. I was concerned about going to sleep with him so close to me. My tiny apartment had a single door that slid out from the wall to separate my main living area from my bedroom, but of course he could fit easily under the door if he wanted to. So I stood up and faced him at the wall. I said that I was now going to sleep and that I would continue to honor him if he could please do the same while I slept. I thanked him for being such a good listener and houseguest, slid the door shut and went to bed. When I opened the door in the morning, there he was still hanging out on the wall where I'd left him.

I went up to him, my face nearly touching the wall, and thought, *I wonder if he's alive?* In that moment he flew off the wall and I never saw him again. I know we saw each other that night. I know he heard me. Whether he left the wall during the night or not, he made sure to be there when I woke up to let me know that he had honored my space. I had no bites on my body anywhere. I felt seen. I felt respected. I felt heard. I believe he felt the same. I believe we can coexist with nature when we make the choice to see into the life that exists inside the bug or creature and honor its presence in this world. There isn't anything alive on this planet that's here in vain. Although we may not know why or understand, every living thing on this planet has purpose here. We can deepen our connection and enhance the quality of our lives by seeking to learn more, honor the space and allow for all God's creatures to live and be as they are.

When you say yes and welcome in new experiences in your life, you really can't be too surprised when God begins to show you manifestations of that. So I had said yes to bugs and welcomed them into my home, right? I said yes to all who felt guided to join me, not just the gentle, pretty-to-look at bugs.

So I couldn't be mad when at four a.m. I went into my bathroom to pee and was blessed to see an enormous sewer roach in my bathtub. These are a pretty normal thing to see in Phoenix if you don't keep your drains covered, especially during the summer months. This sucker was huge! And while I wasn't on board to kill him, I certainly didn't want him in my space either. This variety will take flight if triggered. Hell no! I didn't want that thing flying at me. I'm cringing even now, five years later, just thinking about it.

I stood frozen in my hallway just staring at him, willing him not to move, trying to figure out how I was going to get him out of my apartment. I saw him crawl down the side of the tub between the curtain and the liner. He moved all the way to the bottom of the curtain and all I could see were his antennae wiggling out from underneath. I was crawling out of my skin! I was like, "Dude, you're making me so uncomfortable right now, could you please go back to where you came? I'm not going to hurt you, I just don't want you in my house." He didn't budge. Even his antennae were still. I stood staring at him for what seemed like hours when I finally decided to call my brother-in-law Roland. I felt ridiculous and powerless. I just wanted him out, but I felt such fear around trying to capture him. The thought of him flying at me was more than I could handle.

Roland, being the kindhearted man that he is, said he'd be over as soon as he could to help me take care of it. He was about forty minutes away from my place at the time and on his way into work, so I knew this was putting a pinch on his morning. I had to trust that it was all going to work out for the best, for all of us. While I waited for him to arrive, I decided to talk to the roach again. I told him the truth that Roland would probably find a way to kill him when he got there, instead of just putting him outside. I didn't want that for him so I told him to crawl back down the drain. I kept saying this over and over to him. "I want you to live, dude, crawl back down the drain before he gets here." Sure enough, when Roland got there and we went into the bathroom, the roach was gone. We stripped down the curtain, pulled all the towels, moved everything out of the way, but he was nowhere to be found. We went through the entire apartment looking for him, moving furniture, rugs, everything. No sign of him. He had heard me and listened. I know he did. This was not a small bug by any means and given my small space and minimal furnishings, there was no place for him to hide. I never saw him again, and I smile now thinking that he went on to live his best life, whatever that means in cockroach land. Again, I felt connected, seen, heard, and honored. And if I've learned anything on this crazy ride of mine, it's that life is important, regardless of what it looks like. Life is important. Life matters.

Soon after these incidents occurred, I moved from my apartment and purchased my very first house. As with any new home, I went in and conducted a clearing and blessing ceremony before moving anything in. It is also during this time that I welcome in all spirit forms from the light that feel called to hold space with me. This is when things got really buggy in my world! We suddenly had a cricket hotel scene going on, with crickets going in and out of the house all day long, entire families moving and grooving in our happy little home. I just let them be. My daughter wasn't too thrilled to have them around, but she soon accepted their presence as normal. I remember waking up one morning and while I was cutting into a lemon near the sink, I looked over and there, chilling on top of a bottle of peppermint oil was a chipper-looking grasshopper. He hung out for a couple days then was gone. Praying mantis would visit me from time to time as well outdoors while working in the yard. I loved having the chance to get up close and personal with these bugs because they were teaching me so much about myself. They were teaching me about the value in curiosity, namely, that being curious could take us into a space of healing and learning while removing the fear that typically comes from encountering things of this nature. When (if ever) was the last time you put your face right up to a bug that creeps you out? How did it feel? Would you do it again? What if you knew it could change your life forever in ways that you'd only dreamed about? Would you do it?

Enter the Bees

I looked down at my lap. My arms were cradling a newborn-sized bee. Snuggling deeply into my breast, gazing up at me, big, beautiful, bee eyes. Had I just given birth? What was I looking at? Was it me, being reborn? How on earth am I seeing this? Before I had time to contemplate further, I was taken on an epic, crazy adventure that I'm still trying to wrap my brain around.

What if you sat down one day, closed your eyes, and suddenly saw yourself looking out through the eyes of a bee?

What if, next thing you know, you're flying through the air, gliding in and out of plants and flowers? You can see all the parts up close – the veins in each leaf, the stems, the beautiful bounty of photosynthesis at work. It's a fantastic feast for your senses. You are the bee, but you are still you as well! As you journey along you are gathering information, expanding your vision, and moving through a space that you could have never imagined. Think it sounds crazy? Well, it's exactly what happened to me in the spring of 2017.

Bees had been following me around for years, loudly interrupting my hikes, landing on my pen while I journaled outside, coming into my house and, on more than one occasion, literally flying beside my car as I drove down the road. I found them frustrating and annoying – quite frankly, a pain in my butt. I just wanted them to leave me alone. It wasn't until after my experience that I realized they were trying to get my attention, and it was time to listen. I was going through a very rough time in my life at this point. I was dealing with some unexplained health issues and feeling as if there was no hope left to feel better. Here is some of the story.

As I said earlier, once upon a time I was a competitive bodybuilder and personal trainer. I entered the world of fitness after spending a lifetime being told and thinking that I was fat. I began in 2003 with running my first half marathon. I was hooked! I immediately signed up for a full marathon (completed in 2005) and joined a gym. I walked in my first day and told the trainer, "I just want to be a better runner. Can you help me train for that?" She opened the door to a whole new world for me. I was watching my physical body transform right before my eyes. I suddenly had confidence too! I could now walk into a room regardless of what I was wearing or feeling and know that I could handle myself no matter what. I finally understood what it meant to feel good in my skin. I was learning so much on this journey. My nutrition became like a second job. I was constantly researching and experimenting with things in my body, some food, some supplements. I also was experimenting with removing things that I'd eaten my entire life, like gluten-based products and dairy. I was learning how to tune into my body in deeper ways to really hear what She needed. I loved the person I was becoming!

All this started to change in 2006 when I had breast implants put in. As a competitor, it seemed like the next logical step to my success. So many women had them and I found myself just wanting to feel more feminine inside my athletic body. (Notice I said inside?) I didn't understand back then that loving the self was an inside job. I thought I was loving myself when I said yes to the surgery – I would learn that later – and I loved my new boobs! I loved them so much! I finally felt sexy, womanly, and more importantly, I finally felt I had what I needed to win my competitions. What resulted instead was something completely different.

At first, the signs of Breast Implant Illness seemed fleeting. I could always pass off the pain, brain fog, stomach issues as overtraining and not getting proper nutrition. Even when the symptoms continued, I didn't pay much attention to them. In keeping up with the hormone management and proper nutrition, my body was always trying to get my attention about something. Fast forward to 2016, when I was preparing for a competition in November. Sometime around September or October I woke up and saw that one of my implants had ruptured. I initially thought that my leaning out process had taken hold as I was so close to the show date. What this means is that the closer it gets to showtime, the leaner the body becomes, and drastic, overnight changes are not uncommon. Dropping noticeable inches, pounds, or visible cellulite during the night is a normal part of contest preparation. The body engages in incredible, organic processes in preparation for a competition. I knew there was nothing I could do between then and the show to take care of the rupture, so I just let it be. My custom-made suit needed to be altered even more now to support the ruptured breast.

It wasn't until April of the following year that I was financially able to take care of the repair. Insurance companies won't touch an elective surgery like this, even though I had a defective product. I implanted with silicone gummies this time, thinking they would hold up better than the saline variety. This is when my life really took a turn. My previous symptoms cranked way up and a bunch more new symptoms came out to play. I suddenly had joint/muscle pain that made me feel like I was ninety. It got so bad that I had to cut off my hair because I couldn't hold my arms up over my head to dry or style it. This pain kept me in bed many days, barely able to move. My back was going out regularly. I was missing so much work, and on the days when I did make it in, I couldn't make it through my shift without taking a nap on my break. My brain fog went from mildly annoying to full-blown cognitive dysfunction. I couldn't properly discern my body in physical space, so I would hit my head or knock my knees or face into things after misjudging their placement. I had to remove the rubber mat I stood on at work because anything other than flat floor under my feet made me feel like I was going to fall over. I stuttered and stumbled over words that I just couldn't remember anymore. I couldn't breathe well and simple chores like taking out the trash became unbearable. I had no idea what was happening inside my body. I was a shell of myself. I couldn't exercise anymore and ended up putting on sixty lbs. It didn't matter what I ate. I was drinking a lot too. It helped with the pain and kept me from focusing on the fact that I felt that I'd lost myself. I was terrified of what was happening inside my body, but I had such a fear of doctors and western medicine. The only thing I knew to do was to pray.

My answered prayer came in the form of a woman at work, who up until that point, I found extremely triggering. Funny how life surprises you like that. She and I happened to be working in the same department one day and a superficial conversation suddenly turned to breast implants. She told me she had them and proceeded to tell me about the decline of her health. My wheels were definitely spinning now. I hung on her every word! She asked me if I'd heard of Breast Implant Illness, which I hadn't. She shared that saline and silicone implants both leached toxins into the body, shutting down every system and making women sick. She then gave me the name of two Facebook groups that support women suffering from these symptoms. I went home that night and jumped into these groups. I cried reading their stories. They matched my own. Healthy lives suddenly turned upside down, families broken apart, women wanting to end their own lives. I had come to the end of my rope as well. I could no longer live with the pain, nor did I want to. It was clear what I had to do – get these things out of my body as soon as possible – but Dear God, how was I going to afford another out-of-pocket surgery when I was still paying on the other one?

From that moment in April 2018 when I made the decision to get my implants removed, God began orchestrating every detail, down to each miraculous dollar that flowed in to help me pay for it. On May 1, 2019, I had my third breast surgery. This experience alone showed me that a higher power exists and will fully support our best interests; we just have to make the decision. Thank. You. God!!

Every day since has been a beautiful reminder that nothing is more important than my health. I thought I was doing all the right things. And I was, to the degree that I was informed. The medical system that supports implant surgery does not support informed consent; at least it doesn't at this point. I have met and befriended some extraordinary women who are doing incredible work to change the system so women at least have all the info they need to make the best decision for themselves. I don't regret having implants, because I love how deeply I love myself now. I didn't know how to do that before getting them. I'm not angry anymore, I just want to share my story in the hopes that other women will love themselves enough to hold sacred the body they have and not alter it with surgery and toxins. It's hard enough living in a toxin-filled world without adding more to it.

There are so many layers to this story. I continue to see myself in new ways and appreciate the way my body has supported me even through my darkest hours. I can no longer take for granted the softness of my femininity, hugging someone with my whole heart and feeling deep, healing breath move through my body. Because of the implants, I had to lose myself and all the superficial attachments in order to find the woman I was always meant to be. I still have residual symptoms that can usually be managed with good nutrition and lots of movement. Life is beautiful again! I can smile. And my long, wild curls are making a comeback.

I am here to support anyone who has or knows someone with implants and is having any questionable health issues. This is a no-judgment zone, so all stories are welcome. The journey of loving the self is deeply sacred and cannot be judged by anyone. I see you. I love you. Thank you for sharing in my story.

So how does this relate to my connection to bees? I believe in the deepest part of my being that it was the bees who helped me to figure out what was causing my health issues. It was the guidance of my spirit team and guardian angel speaking to me through the bees about the toxicity inside my body.

Unless I had to be at work, I hid in my house most days. I was in so much physical pain I couldn't bear to do anything more than lay on the couch or in bed. But my guides would coax me outside, a little bit every day. The bees were there to welcome me with open arms. Always. Each day I would spend a little more time outside with them. I started to notice things shifting inside my body. I started to feel at peace, at ease, and my pain lessened enough to let me breathe. I couldn't explain what was happening, but the time between when I discovered the implants were causing me to be sick and the surgery to have them removed, so many magical things took place. So much love and support showed up, new friends, unexpected gifts of cash to help pay for the surgery, I felt a clarity and confidence about life that I've not ever felt before. I felt I finally had hope! And even though I was still dealing with debilitating pain, I felt so secure and grounded within myself. It's like for the first time ever I finally understood what it meant to trust myself. I trusted life. And even though I didn't know what was coming down the path, I wasn't afraid. There is something so beautifully empowering and grounding about not fearing the unknown. I'd never known that feeling before, and it was pretty incredible! I know that being outside immersed in nature and connecting deeply with the bees was healing me. I know down to my bones.

I still remember the day a bee came into my house. I was anxiously trying to get him outside without harming him or getting stung in the process. And in that moment, when I was so freaked out, I suddenly heard very clearly in my mind, "Why are you running away from yourself?" Something in those words hit down to my bones. From that day on, every time a bee invaded my space, I would be still and listen. Don't get me wrong, though, I resisted like crazy! I had never been stung and I certainly didn't want to start now. But even deeper than that was an incredible fear that surged through my being. It felt paralyzing. Have you ever felt this fear? Where does it come from? Why is it so overpowering? These questions and so many others rolled through my mind. The only way I was going to find out was to welcome the fear and sit with the bees.

I started with baby steps. I made wonder and curiosity my new best friends and just showed up. I believe this step alone was the most powerful and created the most momentum in my quest. I quickly learned that the more I sat still and listened, the less fear I felt. Are you willing to show up for yourself and find out what the bees want to share with you? Let's get started then!

Step 1: Invitation/Visualization

Inviting the bees into your world is a very brave first step. This can be done at night before sleep, to have them enter your dreams. If this is the way that feels best to you, keep a journal and pen close by to make note of your dreams immediately upon waking, even before you get out of bed. You can also invite them anytime during the day, wherever you are. Bees are diligent messengers of the natural world. They will hear you no matter where you are and what words you use; they will even hear you through your fear and doubt. Bees are attracted to a pure and gentle heart, you need only approach with sincerity and kindness. Visualizing a single bee or group of bees is also a great way to connect with their energy. This can be done simultaneously with the invitation process. You'll need to find a quiet space to sit or lay down. Close your eyes, take in a few slow, deep breaths, and visualize your bee guides.

In either of these methods you can have a question ready that you would like to have them answer, or you can just ask them what message they have for you. We live in a loud, busy world. Communicating with the natural world requires immense patience and trust if its new to you. It also requires consistent practice. Make it a point to connect with your bees daily, even if just for a few minutes. I've found that telepathy is their primary means of relaying information to you. It may sound like your own thoughts in the beginning, but the more times you reach out to them, the better you'll be able to distinguish their voice from your own. Some of the ways that messages come through for me is through specific song lyrics suddenly playing over and over in my head (especially songs I've not heard in years), movie quotes, billboards, license plates, or even straight-up voices speaking out of the blue. I even hear different languages and accents from time to time. Over time, you will build a strong rapport with your guides and you will know without a doubt what they are trying to say to you. Once you feel at ease here, move on to Step 2.

Step 2: Sitting at a Window and Watching Them Work

You'll need to find a quiet space, this time in front of a window looking directly out at a tree or bush where bees hang out during the day. Pull up a comfortable chair and get as close to the window as possible. The idea here is to really see the bees and how they operate. Getting a closer look allows you to see the life inside of them and how they show up for humanity. There is much to learn from bees and the more we see them for their magic, the more we can honor them as an integral part of this world. So, just as you did in Step 1, sit quietly, eyes open this time, take in a few deep breaths, and have your question ready. Again, when you feel ready, move on to Step 3.

Step 3: Sitting Outside Directly Front/Center of Their Favorite Tree or Bush

Note: Working with bees is about honoring space. If you are allergic, please honor yourself and stick to the first two steps. If you really want to stare your fears down, choose another insect. This method can be done with any bug or animal that calls to you.

I have a robust, red lantana bush in front of my house that is packed with bees daily. I sit on the walkway in front of it, with bees flitting less than an inch from my face. While you do not have to sit with them this close to you, do choose a location that allows you to get as close as possible. You may need a yoga mat or pillow for comfort. This position can be triggering, so be patient with yourself. Take slow, deep breaths to calm and center. You may notice your heart racing. You may feel the urge to run or swat them away. Sit with this discomfort. Just sit with it. Stillness and willingness to look beyond the fear make miracles happen.

Some questions to consider while sitting with the bees:

- What are your greatest fears?
- Where does pain show up in your world?
- In what ways do you feel small and insignificant?
- Where in your life are you out of balance?
- What distractions keep you from taking action on your dreams?
- What one small thing can you do today to make this world a better place?
- How can you turn that one thing into a daily practice for even greater impact in the world?

I have spent countless hours in meditation and various forms of communication with the spirit world. But connecting directly with bees has been the most magical experience of my life. It has changed me in beautiful and profound ways. It has the power to change you too! Bees are here to teach us how to become one with our purpose. They ask us to claim our most potent self, breathe life into our gifts, and come out of hiding.

Who would you "bee" without your fear? Are you ready to find out?

Wednesday, September 29, 2021

This morning I awoke with the energy of the spider around me. Like, just the feeling that I had a spider with me. It's so weird that even now I feel these things so deeply and yet don't know what to do with the information. I took it as my guides trying to speak to me through spider. So here we are. When I think of trying to explain how it feels to feel the energy of a bug around me, it's like seeing it when it's not there in physical form. And while it may be there in physical form, it's not showing itself, and therefore I only feel its presence.

Back to the spider energy…I had actually felt it when I went to bed last night, almost like I could feel a spider watching me. I've gotten to the point that this stuff is not creepy any-more…well, most times. I have to watch my thoughts about it. If I let them take me down a fearful rabbit hole then I ab-solutely start getting creeped out. But if I sit in a space of curiosity with it then something more beautiful emerges. There's always an awareness, an element of clarity or some odd little bit of fun that comes when I sit in the energy of my bugs. I can't say that I willingly call out to them, it usually looks like me praying for guidance then having my guides show up as the spider, the bee, whoever feels called in that moment. But they know they are welcome, they know I will hear them, feel their presence, and they know that I will listen, because well, I've learned that when I don't listen, life gets hard. Life gets tricky. Things start to breakdown; I feel ungrounded and chaotic. Stress manifests, irritation sets in and then I forget how to see all the beautiful things around me that show me just how blessed and abundant I am. I forget to notice the butterflies dancing around my face trying to get me to laugh, I forget to notice all the little things that remind me that this life is a magical fucking carpet ride and the only time it's not fun is when I'm forgetting to notice the little things. Spider is trying to channel a message right now. Let's see what he has to say.

Ahhhh creative one, thank you for hearing my call. I am so happy you have joined me this morning. Your creativity is a gift to this world and you mustn't let your niggling little thoughts get in the way of your greatness. Imagine them as tiny baby spiders falling down over the top of your head and onto your neck. You feel the chaos, the irritation, the fear of all of them going everywhere willy nilly. You have no control over where they go and that creates even more of them, creating more chaos in your mind. Your mental chatter and fearful little what-ifs are keeping you from fully embracing your creative talents. You mustn't get stuck in the web of your own thoughts. It will wrap you up and suffocate the very breath out of you. You are very aware child, very aware indeed, you have the capacity to change this situation for yourself at any moment. Begin employing your own advice. You write it with such conviction and grace…now let yourself experience that, over and over and over again. That is how you will create the life you dream of. {5:55a.m.} I believe in you.

For those of you who are into numerology or connect with the energy of numbers, the number five signifies change. A string of fives is a very clear message that great change is either happening now or about to happen. Change is not something to fear, even when we don't like it. It's another one of those elements to look on with curiosity. I used to fear change, so much. Now I embrace it, and life has become much easier to navigate. Life is still hard, for sure, but change doesn't have any power over me. It has no power over you either. You are in control of how you respond to anything causing discomfort in your world. Embrace change! You will thank yourself for it.

WRITING AS MEDICINE

Working with the faery realm has taught me the importance of seeing the truth of what lives in my heart and giving voice to it without apology. I believe that, next to our heart, our voice is the most powerful thing we possess. It can be challenging to let the magic of our heart out for the world to hear. This is one of the great lessons of faery guidance. You must share your truth. You must. It's what you came to earth to do. Your soul is here on purpose to live and speak truth. One of the most potent and profound ways that I've learned how to acknowledge and honor my voice and share the message that God has laid on my heart is through writing. Writing is medicine for the soul. It soothes the scared, silent voice within that longs to be heard. It creates a safe, sturdy container to cultivate courage, inner power, and freedom. You have spent a lifetime biting your tongue, stuffing down words and wisdom, working like hell to only be seen and not heard. Before you read any further, I want you to hear this: your words matter, your thoughts and feelings are important, and the stories living inside your body deserve to be shared and honored.

I have been writing for as long as I can remember. I wrote a short story in the third grade titled "The Talking Clock." It was twelve pages long, and for a nine-year-old, that was a lot! I don't remember if I received any positive feedback from my teacher, or even what grade I received, but I do know that I felt so proud of my work! Holding the pages in my hands felt like gold, a joy I'd never experienced before. Something birthed inside of me that day, a knowing, a vision, that one day I'd be a bestselling author. I also learned to read at the tender age of three. The memory of sitting with my grandma at the kitchen table with her loving guidance and teaching feels as real as if it's happening right now. I often wonder if her love of teaching and reading is what sparked my own. I fell in love with books and language. I loved building my vocabulary with big, bodacious words. It was filling my cup in a way that I couldn't explain. I didn't know this at the time, but I was preparing myself, nurturing my purpose, and building a support system that I would need years down the road.

I grew up in a house where self-expression was allowed and celebrated, but only if it didn't anger my dad. He and I did not have a healthy relationship by any means. I used to joke that all I had to do was take my first breath to trigger his anger. As sensitive as I was, I could feel everything going on, every negative thought and emotion, in that house, though at the time I didn't know that's what was happening.

When my body had had too much, it would begin to release in a flood of adolescent emotion. This is where self-expression became the slow spiral dance into the disappearance of my spirit. My emotions were too much for my dad. His anger raged in response. I was no longer his daughter in need of support, but now a "moody bitch who needed to get the fuck out of his face." I descended, quickly. I put my head down and shut my mouth. I no longer felt safe to express anything in my home. I started hanging out with older kids who I felt supported by. They accepted me exactly as I am, no questions asked. But they also taught me to drink. They showed me drugs. They touched me, and I let them. I felt at home in their presence. I was fourteen years old now and couldn't care less.

But when the sun went down and I could no longer hide under the cloak of fake friends, I went home. I went straight up to my room, turned on some favorite Depeche Mode and pulled out my journal. Writing had become my medicine, the tonic I needed daily to calm my inner battle. I used pencils only; freshly sharpened number twos were my favorite, but really any would do. To the feel the scratch of lead across the page was like a hug from heaven, bringing thought into form right before my eyes. I could move incredible emotion with that pencil, like magic scrawls across all space and time, grounding myself into the bones of my pain. Paper and pencil love me unconditionally. I could rage across the page, fight my demons, spit on my parents, and still there she was holding me, soothing me, whispering into my being, "Keep going baby girl, everything's going to be okay, I promise."

Writing was also my mama bear. She protected me fiercely, guarded my heart, and roared from her bones to anyone that tried to harm me. I found wisdom in her belly, warmth in her words, and I trusted her completely. My own mom was born of courage and grace, and she did her very best to keep the peace between me and my dad. But she hadn't discovered the mama bear that lives inside of her yet, so her gentle ways were no match for the toxic energy that swirled through our house. She too had grown up in a house where she was to be seen and not heard. I needed her to stand up and roar for me, but she couldn't yet. So on I wrote.

There is such a resistance that shows up when we decide to put our voice out into the world. I get it! This book has been over ten years in the making because of my procrastination and other nonsense that kept me distracted. It's truly a labor of love. Whether you want to pen a bestseller or just write to free your heart, it must become a practice, a sacred space you show up for yourself regularly. As with any practice, you will need to give yourself permission to feel through all the thoughts and feelings that will most certainly arise to try and keep you from succeeding. Be gentle with yourself as you move through this process. You are setting your voice free from a lifetime of silence, so it is going to take enormous patience, compassion, and reassurance. Your voice needs to know it is safe to come out. It needs to know you are going to be there for it to support it, no matter how She chooses to express herself. I am going to take you through three of my favorite ways to show up for your voice that will ease you into a space that will allow you to open up the creative channel inside of you. Before we begin, you are going to want to find a place in your home, office, or outdoors to set up your workspace. This part is important because it needs to be a spot you will enjoy going to each day. Make sure it is clean and clutter-free. Your comfort is what's key here. It doesn't matter where you sit or how you sit, as long as you are at ease. Bring in any items that inspire you, keep you focused and bring a cheery, peaceful vibe to the space. Purchase your favorite pencils or pens, notebooks, or journals that catch your eye. Remember this is your space, you can create it in whatever way works best for you. Once your space is ready to go, you are ready to write!

The first method we are going to look at uses the prompt I AM. I AM is one of the most powerful phrases you can ever think, speak, or write. The body has the incredible capacity to respond to your thoughts and words whether you speak them aloud or not. The energy of these words allows you to claim truth inside your body, your cells responding, replicating, expanding, creating change within and around you, so it makes sense to choose words that are affirming, empowering, and loving. Below are some examples of I AM statements that I love working with.

I am worthy.

I am successful.

I am healthy, energetic, and alive!

I am confident and courageous.

I am at peace with my world.

I am in love with my life.

I am willing to change.

I am ready to share my voice.

I am deserving of great love.

I am lovable.

I am safe.

I am a magnet for money.

I am prosperous in all areas of my life.

As you begin to work with I AM statements you may notice resistance or feel triggered. This is normal. If you find yourself writing a statement that does not feel completely true for you, your body will tell you. I invite you to sit with the discomfort of these feelings and write the words anyway. Painful triggers are only our body's way of letting us know areas in our life that are in need of healing and love. So as uncomfortable as it is, be willing to sit with it and keep writing. Sharing your voice has the power to move this emotion out of your body. I will address other ways to move negative emotion out of your body in a later chapter. Working with these prompts alone has the capacity to drastically change your life for the better. Are you ready to tap into the power of your I AM?

Another way to jumpstart your writing process is to create a gratitude list. This method is similar to using the I AM prompts in that you are drawing your attention to things you are thankful for which will begin to shift the chemistry inside your body. We are creative beings and focusing our thoughts on things that are abundant in our lives has the power to once again drastically change our life for the better. One of the magical secrets of the Universe can be found when you give thanks for something you don't yet see in your life. Let's say you're having some financial setbacks causing you to be short on your monthly bills. Start giving thanks for all the money in your bank account. Express gratitude for being able to pay all your monthly bills on time each month. This is a powerful mode of manifesting. It's tricky though because having money problems is very stressful for anyone, but you want to keep your focus on the abundance of all that you have, even if you don't quite have it yet. So you will feel triggered by this when you begin. Sometimes it can be hard to find things to be grateful for when life seems to be crumbling beneath your feet. If this is the case for you, begin with simple, easy to identify things in your world.

I am grateful for my breath.

I am grateful to see another sunrise.

I am grateful for the mess in my house.

I am grateful for my family, my children.

I am grateful for my health.

I am grateful for my ability to smile.

I am grateful for running water.

I am grateful for the food I have to eat.

I am grateful my car is working well.

I am grateful to have friends to connect with.

I am grateful a source greater than myself exists to support me.

I am grateful for my struggles.

I am grateful for the capacity and willingness to change.

Pay attention to how you begin to feel after working with your gratitude statements. Once you move through the discomfort of the initial triggers, you will begin to feel a lightness in your being. Life will begin to feel better and your struggles will feel less stressful. This is how it starts! The gratitude is shifting your vibration to a higher level which will begin to bring material things into your physical reality, so keep going!

I remember many times having no more than five dollars in my bank account and nothing in my wallet, and feeling incredibly abundant and prosperous, as if I had all the money in the world. One day in particular, I remember laughing out loud as I drove down the road because I was so in love with life and feeling so amazing and I had nothing in my bank account and bills still needed to be paid. I was working at the time, but my checks were slim, and money was extraordinarily tight. Yet the pressures of life causing me to suffer so much were nowhere to be seen.

Another perk you may notice when you begin working with daily gratitude is that life becomes better in all areas. So if you're really struggling through your finances right now and using gratitude, don't be surprised if you meet the man or woman of your dreams, or receive the job offer you've been praying for. Gratitude is a magic that soaks into your entire being. This means that your entire life is on track for an upgrade. Now how does that sound?

I also like to do a variation of this technique which involves writing a letter to yourself about things that you expect to attract and be grateful for. Sometimes I've found it hard to just come up with statements of gratitude that I can really feel inside my body. I love the idea of writing a letter because it automatically feels more personal and therefore easier to feel on the inside, which is what we are going for. Shifting the inner vibe is what is going to fuel your outside experience. So if it feels fake trying to come up with statements of gratitude, try this technique instead. Below is a letter I wrote to myself on a day where I was struggling to find some goodness in my world.

Dear Self,

Today is a beautiful day to be me, a beautiful day to tune into the energy around me and move from a place of gentle flow.

There is so much magic to experience! I expect outrageous miracles today. I expect love and prosperity, laughter and joy. I expect today to be a beautiful reflection of all the goodness that lives inside me. I see love. I feel love. I am love.

I breathe deeply through any uncertainty and confusion. I open my heart to receive only good things, healthy things, things that fill me with life. And I surrender very easily those things not for my highest good.

Thank you, Divine Spirit of heaven and earth, for guiding me today, protecting me today, and helping me remain steeped in your love. GRATITUDE, GRATITUDE, GRATITUDE!

All my love,

Erin Christine

A third way to tap into the medicine of your voice is what I like to call Name that Emotion. Sit down in your workspace and think about a negative emotion you've been feeling lately. Can you name it? What are you feeling? Where in your body are you feeling it? What would you like to say to this emotion? Be as specific as you can with your thoughts, then pick up your pencil and at the top of your page write the words "Dear Anger," or whatever emotion you're feeling, then pen a letter to the emotion.

The following is a powerful letter I wrote to my emotions in 2018:

My Dear Beloved Emotions,

I hate you! I fucking hate you! You come in all badass like you own the joint and push me around. You are heavy and brutal and you hurt my being. You stir up so much inside of me that feels so fucking uncomfortable; sadness, confusion, loneliness, doubt, anger, rage, a collective "FUCK YOU" to the world in which I walk. Why do you have to feel so bad? Why must I have to feel you, this bloody fucking rubbish of emotion?

But then I remember who you are and why you must be a part of my life. You stir shit up, that's for damn sure! But when the dust settles, I can see clearly things that I couldn't before. I have incredible clarity and peace of mind. I also notice that this badass energy you come blowing in here with all the time is rubbing off on me BIGTIME! Every time you leave me, I look in the mirror and I gaze on a stronger, lovelier version of myself. My voice is powerful now and I'm not afraid of its magnitude. I used to run from it and now I revel in it. My words are wiser and my actions are intentional and filled with grace. The strength that I gain from you is blowing my fucking mind. I feel like there isn't anything I can't handle in this life. I've seen it all and heard it all, and when something comes at me and kicks me in the gut, I stop and remember my power and I take a breath. And then I take another, and another. And when the dust settles once again, there I am, still standing, a pillar of ridiculous fucking strength and grace.

I am a sight to behold! Shoulders back, heart open, head up, eyes bright and curious…an energy of fiery truth blazing from my cellular being. I marvel at myself. I am a miracle! The way I am so willing to burn myself down and rebuild, over and over and over again. This burning down of self creates a forest within me, a living, breathing ecosystem of thought and blood claiming my space in this world.

I see you, emotions, and I honor you in all your rudeness and stink. I stand before you as one, a merging of cellular grace, we will continue to move in sync until my breath expires and we are released in freedom to dance in the ethers. I love you! I'm sorry. Please forgive me. Thank you.

I was beside myself when this letter bubbled up out of me. I scrawled across the page like a mad fool and let my words be as they needed without criticism or judgment. This is a pivotal piece when using writing as a tool for healing. It must be a censor-free zone. Loving the parts of ourselves that we hate is an incredible act of self-love. This act alone can create a gateway to healing. This entire experience took fifteen, maybe twenty minutes max, and by the time I finished my body and mind were both at peace. I was exhausted, but I had moved a massive amount of pain in a very short time. I don't even remember what had triggered the reaction in me. That's the beautiful thing about healing wounds and moving the energy out of our body, we don't need to know what it is. If we do – great! – but it's not necessary to experience a full healing release. And because I released all this on paper, I had nothing but peace and ease to take home to my daughter that day.

Writing is a gateway to truth. We all have profound and beautiful truth living inside of us and most, if not all, is longing to be released. When I say profound and beautiful truth, I mean incredible pain and struggle. Our lives are fraught with tragedies and ugliness but bringing it to light and letting it all breathe makes it sacred and beautiful. Writing is a safe container for the thoughts we hold deep in our bones. It's an avenue to voice the unspeakable. For me, it's always been a way of reminding myself of who I am and what I came to this planet to do. What truth is longing to be voiced from inside of you? Are you willing to let it out? How would it feel to voice the unspeakable and finally set yourself free?

Elemental Journeys

I was chosen to tell this story; or, as a soul in the ethers, I chose to incarnate into this body during this time and space to tell this story. Either way, I now know the enormity of this message. I now understand why things had to show up as they have and continue to do so. I feel as if I've seen and heard everything the Universe has to offer, and yet, I'm still awed almost daily by Spirit and my work with the faery realm. My message was birthed in magic and mystery. I have been challenged with the task of bringing the work of Fae down to earth for people to have a better understanding of how to create their own flow of magic and miracles. It seems almost comical to think about bringing the Fae message down to earth when that is everything they are. It seems so obvious to me the way they operate and keep this planet going, but most folks have forgotten the roots of their birth and how we are a unified one of all creation. We bear a grave responsibility for the upkeep and care of this beloved planet, and quite frankly we are failing miserably. We've forgotten what it means to be a dutiful steward of the Earth, abundant in all resources. We consume and destroy, consume and destroy, consume and destroy. It's a dark, heavy cycle that keeps our beautiful earth in a constant state of emergency trying to renew and repair. That's why this message is of high priority. I am but one voice, but I trust the Universe to awaken the other voices and call forth in courage to share in the healing of this planet. It begins with healing ourselves. It begins with opening our eyes and heart, seeing the truth of our existence here and having the courage to walk in alignment with that truth. Your voice is needed now more than ever. Read on, dear friends. You are on the right path.

In order for me to prepare myself for the task of bringing this message to the masses, I had to be initiated into experiences to expand my awareness, clarify my visions and solidify the message of Fae into my bones. In truth, the wisdom already existed inside of me. The initiations were merely set up to help me remember my place in the world, my mission, and the steps I would need to take to see it to completion. I call them initiations, but really they were spiritual journeys to the lower world where I could train in the ways of the ancient ones, the keepers of the land. When I say keepers of the land, I am referring to the keepers of the planet. It is here that I was grounded in ritual, alchemy, shapeshifting, the nature of energy and how to manage my own, my gifts of spiritual sight, telepathy, and feeling things inside my body. As we move through this chapter, you may notice a shift in the language or tone of my words; this is because much of what I share here is channeled straight from Source. I will clarify which energies are speaking through me and format the communication in italics for better understanding. As you read through my passages, I'd like to invite you to pay very close attention to the channeled information. Tune into your body and see how the energy feels. It may help to close your eyes and breathe deeply placing a hand over your heart. See if you can feel the difference in each of the voices. How does the energy feel inside your body? This is a great way to begin working deeper with elemental guides. Learning to discern the energy will give you clues and clarity to who exactly is trying to connect with you. Remember, intention is key. Ask for a specific energy and see if you can feel it when it arrives. Is it male or female? Is it a single voice or a collective voice? Don't be afraid to ask questions. Spirit wants to draw you closer and rejoices in all attempts to reach out and communicate. You are so very loved, safe, and supported through this process. It's important that you know this.

Merlin is coming forth to speak first. I've been channeling Merlin for ten-plus years now and it's crazy how real he is in my world. I admit, I still feel disbelief for so much of what I experience, but once you let Spirit in, they're not leaving, especially when they know you've got an important purpose to commit to. So when Merlin began showing up for me, I really thought I was going nuts. I could hear the energy of his voice reverberate through my being like that of a stern yet loving grandfather. He communicates from a place of tough love. He is my grandmaster of sorts in the lower world, overseeing all my lessons and journeys. He takes this work very seriously and doesn't put up with any bullshit. And let's face it, as humans we come with lots of bullshit. My personal bullshit is of epic proportions. He knows this and he operates accordingly. He knows I strive to be the best I can be so he communicates in a way that helps me respond best to his demands. He also understands that this is not an easy task to follow through on. It has taken me decades to build the courage and confidence to even write these words here. Spirit only asks that we show up in the best way we know how. We are supported every step of the way, but we have to show up, even when we are afraid and have no clue what we're doing.

Here I am talking to Merlin, my grandmaster, grandfather spirit guide who watches over me and teaches me how to communicate this message to you, dear reader.

I am Merlin. I am recruiting those ready and willing to share the message of healing for our planet. But ready and willing you must be! You begin where you are and learn as you go. I prepare assignments that are designed to stretch you in body, mind, and spirit. You will learn the ways of the land and merge yourself with the consciousness of all that is. You are fully capable and equipped to handle everything I lay before you. You will feel fear. You will feel doubt. You will feel confusion. You will feel pain and be steeped in darkness at times. But you will also feel light, freedom, life, and love like you've never experienced. If you are feeling the call to go deeper into the healing of this planet, and therefore deeper into the healing of yourself, I am here to assist you. You need only call my name to your side. Even just thinking my name will call forth my magic to merge with your magic. Yes, you have magic. If you are ready to heed the call, I will teach you how to use it mindfully for the greater good of the entire Universe. Did you know you were that powerful? It's time you knew how powerful a being you truly are. I am a support system for you as you explore this new adventure. Treat it as an adventure, dear child. Your life truly will never be the same. You must be willing to summon courage from within that perhaps you've never experienced. You must be willing to trust me in all things and in turn trust yourself. Your guidance is true and real, but it won't all make sense right away. It takes time to undo old programming and deep con-ditioning that has kept you asleep all these years. But you are here, wide awake, thinking my name, Merlin, reading my message, you are ready! Yes, you are! It is time for your voice to be heard. Your gifts are unique and therefore your assignments will be catered to your personal blueprint of consciousness. What this means is that you incarnated with a specific DNA, a blueprint of your passion, your purpose. This imprint is locked into universal consciousness therefore there is no way for you not to complete your mission here on earth. Even when you lose track, fall off your path, and make every mistake in the book, you are always moving in the direction of your purpose. You will always be led back to where you need to be. You can make this easier on yourself though by connecting to me and your spirit team as often and as deeply as possible. We are here to support you every step of the way. You may not always see or hear us, but we are here. Know this! You need only say my name, Merlin, or call out the name of your other guide or guides. You will have many on your path. Get to know them. They are your spirit family. It is time dear child. It is your time. Do not let another moment pass by. In humble service and gratitude, Merlin.

So much of the work we do with Spirit involves going deep into the different realms of consciousness, and when we return, we have no recollection of the experience. But the work is imprinted in our DNA. Our unique blueprint is updated each time we dig deeper into our consciousness. This is why nothing you do is ever in vain. It all counts, even the mistakes. Doesn't it feel good to know that you are perfect in your humanness? You may notice yourself speaking differently or behaving in new ways, this is how you know that Spirit is getting through to you. You need not remember all the details to be and feel successful in your soul work. Trust yourself. Your soul is well versed on what's best for you in this life. But there will be many times when you will be gifted vivid memories of your experiences. I believe that these are the moments you are to share with the world. Your experiences become part of your new story and hold great value for the collective consciousness. This is where it becomes vital for you to share your story. There is someone out there praying to connect with a person who knows what you know, a person who has been through what you've been through. It is through your story that you become a light in someone else's darkness. You make sense of their chaos and help them to understand their purpose in this world. You are important and your experiences become the gift you are here to share with the world. I am going to take you through some of my most vivid journeys with spirit, the details deeply imprinted on my soul.

Meeting My Dolphin Self

May, 2009

I had just completed my training to become a Transformational Life Coach. I had been connecting with Spirit for several years now and was still seeking, still hungry for anything I could get my hands on to help me understand more about myself. I remember being out one day with a girlfriend who was also heavily into spiritual teachings. We went to a local metaphysical shop to look around, and I told her that I was craving dolphin music. *Yes, literally craving it.* What is dolphin music anyway? I had no idea what I was looking for, but I had a feeling I'd know it when I heard it. I imagined it to be some kind of meditation music, but I wasn't sure how the dolphin aspect would come into play. I made my way over to the section with books and CDs and immediately a CD caught my eye with a man standing waist-high in the ocean with a dolphin under his arm, like he was hugging it! I grabbed the CD and knew instantly it was supposed to be mine. I just knew! I was so excited to listen to this and I had no idea why.

I continued to shop around the store and suddenly felt a strong pull to have a tarot reading done by one of the readers on site. I am very choosy about who I allow to do spirit work with me so I wasn't sure who I would go to. I immediately was drawn to a man sitting at a nearby table, and I had to really trust my guidance on this one because I only liked working with women when it was so deeply personal. Spirit kept telling me that this man was the one. "Go see him," I was told. I sat down at his table, he asked me my name and if I had a question I'd like guidance on. As he shuffled the deck of cards, I told him I was worried about my relationship with my daughter. Inside I was afraid I was going to lose her to her father, who at that time had full custody of her. I was afraid he was going to take her from me. I was struggling financially and had given him custody because I couldn't care for her the way she needed. On paper we had joint custody, and I was allowed to see her whenever I wanted, but it was better for all of us if she stayed under his care at that time. This situation stirred up so much fear in me. Was I even a real mother if I couldn't care for my daughter? Would I ever be able to care for her? Would she even want to be with me? These questions and so many more worried me every day. I sat listening to the man share various messages about the cards he pulled. I hadn't shared with him my specific fears and concerns, I only mentioned that I wanted to know if there was anything for me to know about my relationship with my daughter. He said me to that I would never lose my daughter because she was repaying a karmic debt to me. His words were only slightly comforting. What karmic debt? Would I ever be shown the truth about that? I paid him and walked away feeling sad and disappointed. Spirit had strongly guided me to get a reading from that man and that was all I got? I felt duped!

Ahh well, I thought with a sigh, *I'll get over it.* I purchased my dolphin CD and my friend and I headed out of the store. It wasn't until later that night when I went to run some errands that I popped my new dolphin music into my CD player in my truck. The moment the music started I felt this incredible emotion well up inside of me. There really are no words to explain how it felt, but suddenly I was sobbing, heaving, choking on my tears. I was just shy of pulling off to the side of the road because I thought I was going to have an accident. I took in a deep breath as the emotion settled into my body and suddenly, I had the most overwhelming feeling of love surging through my body. It was a love so beautiful and true; it was a feeling I'd never felt before. And then came the wisdom, the whispers downloading truth into my ear. I was a dolphin in a past life. I was feeling the love of my family. I had brothers and sisters, a mom and dad, and we all loved each other fiercely. We took care of each other and there was never any doubt that we were worthy and wanted in this family. It was the purest, most sacred love I'd ever felt. It was magic, pure magic! As it moved through my body, I found myself smiling, grinning like a fool, then giggling, driving down the road laughing at all this goodness making its way through my being. There was no denying the truth of this experience. The emotion moved through my body like a hurricane on steroids, an energy that could only come from God. There was no way I was making this up. When I finally got to my destination, I sat in the parking lot for the longest time taking in all the moments of that experience.

I grew up in a typically dysfunctional, sometimes abusive family feeling unsupported at best, loathed at worst. Suffice it to say I would've much rather grown up in my dolphin family! I had gotten really good at journaling my experiences since my awakening several years prior, but I had a feeling I'd be remembering this one for a very long time. It has now been twelve years and it still feels like yesterday that I learned this about myself. The details continue to make me smile and that feeling, that pure love, I still haven't felt anything like it since. I received a gift that day.

July, 2009

I was on a trip with my boyfriend at the time. We were traveling up the California coast to spend some time in the San Diego area before making our way up to San Francisco to visit with my family who all lived there. I remember we stopped at Newport Beach one day and made our way down to the beach to set up our spot. My boyfriend had to head back to the car to grab some things we had forgotten. I laid back on my blanket and closed my eyes as he walked away. I remember this immense peace washing over me, and feeling like I was falling asleep. But instead of sleep, I slipped into a trance-like space and suddenly began seeing extraordinary visions. It was like watching a movie play out right in front of me. I saw myself as a dolphin. It is a strange realization to see yourself as an animal and still know that you are looking out of your own eyes. The eyes truly are the windows to the soul. Every time I've done intentional past life work, my eyes remain the same no matter what my face or body looked like. I've seen myself as a wolf, an African man, a native princess, and now was looking on myself as a dolphin. My eyes are the same in all personas. This was blowing my mind!

I remember at one point thinking that my boyfriend had been gone for so long, wondering when he was going to return, but I was frozen in my trance. I couldn't move. I continued to stare at myself in awe of what I was witnessing. Next thing I knew I was swimming out towards something, swimming fiercely. I saw my dolphin sister trapped in a fisherman's net that was sweeping the ocean floor, and she was thrashing about, panicking. I moved quickly and as soon as the net shifts, I push her away with my nose and allow the net to gather me up instead. She is freed.

In this moment I come out of my trance on the beach. The whispers of wisdom softly soothe into my ear, "You sacrificed your life for your sister, your sister, who in this life is your daughter, your beautiful daughter, Savannah Faith. Now, may you understand why you will always be deeply connected to her and as your daughter, she is repaying her karmic debt to you for saving her life." Once again, I lay there and just sobbed. What was all this that was happening? I saw everything with my own eyes. It was another piece to the mystery of me. I couldn't make this up if I tried. I don't know how long I laid there crying. But when the emotion settled down, I felt again this extraordinary peace move gently through my being. I know now that I was in the midst of a great and powerful healing of my spirit. This experience needed no journaling, it has been etched in my heart since that day on the beach.

September 2017

I was enrolled in a massage therapy program at The Southwest Institute of Healing Arts. This day in particular I was laying on a table in a myotherapy class. My partner Jason and I were going to be taking turns learning how to work through a psoas release protocol. Psoas release work is a very powerful healing modality, but it's incredibly invasive and can be very uncomfortable. It works through the lower abdominals and groin area. Jason slowly began palpating my left side. I immediately felt a searing pain cut through my side. He eased up on his touch, but the pain remained. I lay there with my eyes closed, feeling it burn through me. Then I watched as the movie started up again where I left off in July. I saw myself trapped in the net I had just freed my sister from. I was very still knowing that I had sealed my fate when I took her place in the net. I watched myself get hoisted up onto the boat, and while one fisherman unwrapped the net, another came over with a steel spear and stabbed it forcefully into my left flank. I watched myself writhe upwards in pain as the blood gushed out onto the deck; I felt the searing fire rage through my body. I watched the life bleed out of me on that boat and a moment later the pain I had initially felt left my body completely.

I am crying as I write these words. This is the first time I've shared this part of my dolphin experience. Moving through the awareness of this experience has been one of the most profound and awesome aspects of my healing journey. I still can't fully wrap my brain around the fact that this is all part of my truth. Our lives are extraordinary tapestries of consciousness woven with pain, struggle, and tragedy. Throughout this book you hear me say many times that we hold our wounds inside our bodies until the body says it's time to release and heal. Our wounds hold clues to the past. If we are willing to open our hearts to the limitless possibilities of consciousness, we have the capacity to heal lifetimes of pain and trauma.

Meeting My Dragon Guide

When I woke up this morning, I had in my mind that I would be diving into sacred womb healing and discussing how my dragon guide has played an integral part in this work. Not surprisingly, my monthly bleed showed up as well…three days early. The body, mind, and spirit are always working together for the greater good of our evolution. There are going to be some things to process and release through my words today that will move with the blood out of my body, which means it's going to be another magical, mystical day in my world. At the very least, it is my hope to have you look on yourself and all your womanly processes with divine reverence and love. You are a sacred, creative vessel radiating such power; it's time you started to believe it!

I was raised in a house where being a woman and dealing with womanly things, like the monthly bleed, was at best an inconvenience and a bother. Most times though I used it as a time to dive head-first into abject self-loathing and disgust. I felt gross, incredibly awkward, and wanted to hide. I began my cycle at age eleven, much earlier than any other girls in my school, and had fully developed breasts just one year earlier. Physically I was a woman, emotionally I was a child. Because of this, I learned very quickly what people, namely boys and men, expected of me. I attracted attention no matter where I went. Boys made fun of me and groped me every chance they got; men stared, whistled, and lusted after me with their greedy gaze. This was the start of a painful journey where seeking sexual and physical validation from men became my measure of worthiness.

I am struggling to get these words out of my being and onto this page. I see now that there is still healing to be done. There's always healing to be done while we're still breathing on this earth. I am holding this space for you, dear sister, as you look inside yourself at what needs to be brought to light. I am here to remind you that your body is a sacred space, the entire Universe wrapped up in human form.

So how do dragons play into all of this? Just like the Fae, dragons are energy, another level of consciousness that is available to us for wisdom and guidance should we seek it out. Dragon energy began coming into my awareness in the spring of 2018 during another class in my massage therapy program. I was laying on a table during a polarity/reflexology session, my eyes were closed, and I was in a deep trance state, but also fully aware and talking through my experiences with my partner. As he worked on me, I suddenly saw myself as a dragon. Again, like the dolphin experience, looking down on myself with my own eyes, seeing myself in a dragon body. The image made me cry. It was so intensely powerful and overwhelming. In that moment, the dragon inside of me began to speak to my heart.

My dear beloved child, I am here to show you who you are. I am here to rise you from the ashes and birth you into a new being of power and grace. Do not be afraid. We are one. My power is your power. You need not fear your power, ever. Do you understand this? Your power is bestowed upon you for the greater good of all humanity and it's imperative that you embrace it fully and give yourself permission to share it with the world. We are protectors of the land, you and I. I am here to show you who you are. Look up, child, see this now. You are a commanding presence with a fiery voice. You have an extraordinary message to share with the world and I am here as a guide to help you fulfill that purpose. You are a messenger of peace and healing. Your love blankets the planet and acts as a soothing balm. Yes, people fear you. People fear what they do not understand. People fear what they are running from in themselves. Do not let it sway you. Stay on purpose. Just as I am here reminding you of your power, you are

here to remind others of theirs. I am your guide. Call on me at all
times for guidance and support. I will teach you the ways of the
land from the dragon's view. Breathe. The truth of me now lives
in the truth of you.

I returned back to the present moment and stared at my
partner. I told him what I had just witnessed and heard. He
looked on me with unconditional love in his eyes, holding the
space for me in a way that I've never experienced with a man.
I laid there looking at him and for the first time, was
unashamed to let a man see me cry. I had no idea where this
new awareness would take me, but I got up from that table a
changed woman. Something inside of me had shifted. And just
like my dolphin experience, I knew that Spirit would continue
to lead me to a greater understanding of the dragon in my
world.

Since this experience, I've watched myself transform in
beautiful ways, honoring my worth, saying yes to things that
nurture my soul, and giving myself the love that I so desperately was trying to get from others who didn't have a clue
how to love me properly. One of the ways that I've only
recently begun to work with to nurture my womb space is by
having regular yoni steam sessions. This is an ancient healing
practice of sitting over a steaming pot of herbs that permeates
the exterior labia and vagina to flush out toxins and aid in
fertility and reproductive health. The sessions are gentle and
meditative, a beautiful way to nurture your inner goddess and
connect with the deepest part of yourself. In July of 2021 I
scheduled a session that was coupled with a dragon activation

to meet your dragon guide. I could not wait! I knew this was going to be a magical experience!

When the day finally came, I slipped easily into a trance state. My dragon showed herself immediately. She told me her name was Lucille. All I could think was, like Lucille Ball? I quickly learned that she was in fact like the Lucille Ball I remember – lighthearted and loving, but fiery feisty as well. This equated to, I'll love you like crazy, but don't cross me. I felt immediately that this guide had my back no matter what. She would defend me to the death if necessary. I felt that down to my bones. She began showing me things and whispering wisdom into my being. I learned she is the keeper and guardian of my womb space and has been protecting me my entire life. The first thing she showed me was an abandonment wound that had been created when I was four years old. My dad had moved out for a while and I hadn't realized it caused a trauma response in my body. I remember in 2010 having a conversation with him about that time he left. He told me that the only reason he came back was because of my younger sister, who was devastated at his departure and wouldn't stop crying for him. He never said one word about missing me or coming back for me as well. This was a hard truth to hear, but it had manifested in my womb space and was now ready to be released.

Lucille kept on. Suddenly I was having all these memories and visions. I saw a little girl of about four years old, I couldn't see her face, but it felt like it was me. It was summertime and she was squatting over a sprinkler in the grass letting the water tickle her labia. She was giggling and squealing with delight. In the next moment she was being yanked away by her mother and yelled at for what she was doing. I knew in that moment a shame wound had just been born inside of me. The next memory was a clear picture of me as an adult, a student teacher in a kindergarten classroom the last semester of my teaching program. Each day we would begin with all the kids in a circle to do the calendar, sing songs, and plan for our day. One of my little girls would plant herself on her back in the middle of the circle, pull her knees up and over the top of her clothes, gently rub herself between her legs. This happened every single day. I remember just letting her be in that space, not saying anything, or drawing any attention to her. The rest of the kids continued to follow my direction and after a few minutes, she would stop and return to her place in the circle. I never knew if I was doing the right thing by not saying anything, but as an adult now healing through my own wounds of shame attached to pleasure, I realize that as I honored her space, I was also honoring myself. I was allowing for healing to take place within my wounded little girl who was shamed for enjoying the feel of her body. I also realize that I was teaching the other kids to be respectful of this behavior and showing them that it was nothing to be ashamed of. Lucille was guiding me through the reclamation of my four-year-old self and returning to me those pieces of my being that were shattered by shame and feeling unworthy of my father's love. During the time of this healing, I was guided to write a letter to the four-year-old inside me.

Dear Four-Year-Old Me,

I am so sorry, baby girl…this is such a confusing time and it's causing so much pain. Your father has moved out and you blame yourself. You feel like if only you were a better little girl, more behaved, quiet, less messy, that he would want to stay, want to hug you and tell you that it was going to be okay. But he's angry all the time and he just left…gone.

Listen to me, sweet girl…you have done nothing wrong, nothing at all. Your father doesn't know how to handle his anger, and while that's not an excuse for him to treat you this way, he doesn't know any better. But I want you to know that I see you. I see your magnificence, your pure heart, and the light of your innocence. You are a treasure baby girl, a treasure, and don't you let anyone ever tell you different. You have been brought to this world for a grand and perfect purpose. You will come across people who will challenge this in you, push and pull you, and make you feel like you are the cause of all their problems. Pay them no mind, you hear? You are here on Divine purpose and these people, while they may be family and loved ones, are your teachers. They are teaching you sacred lessons of surrender, compassion, and forgiveness. They come with harsh lessons to help you see how valuable you are in this world, that your presence here is invaluable.

You are so precious, child, and I know you hurt. But I want you to know that you are safe now and so very supported. You have so many people surrounding you daily that love and cherish you. This world truly wouldn't be the same without you here. It's important that you understand that. I also want you to know and understand that your feelings are nothing to be afraid of. It is safe for you to express yourself in whatever way you see fit. Nobody can hurt you anymore.

I am so proud of you, baby girl! You are so brave! It takes so much courage to feel the pain you've experienced. You have been blessed with such strength and even though you are so young, you still show up as a very brave little girl. You are to be celebrated! I celebrate you today, every day, for you have shown me what it means to shine my light unapologetically, and with all the love and grace you can muster. You are safe, my love. You are safe to be as you are, speak as you are, show up as you are, you are safe always. Never forget that!

I am here for you if you ever need to crawl up into my lap and snuggle in close. You can bring all your feels and sit in my space. I'm here for you, today and always.

All my love, sweet girl,

Your Forty-Six-Year-Old Self

One of my favorite dragon journeys happened several years ago in Colorado, though I didn't know it was the work of dragons until July 2021. I was visiting my best friend and her family for the week and had decided to go out for a run. She lives in a small farming town in the northern part of the state which translates to lots of long, country roads as far as the eye could see. It was the perfect place to run. I set out with only my phone for music and emergencies. I was not a new runner so I felt completely at ease with just myself.; however, I wasn't all that familiar with her neighborhood yet so I planned to stay on the main road.

This run felt amazing, so light, so free. My body felt so at ease as I moved down the road. I ran for what I thought to be a couple miles and decided to turn around to make my way back to the house. A straight shot down the road, no problem. I kept running in the direction of her house and it never came. I kept looking around trying to figure out where I was and I had not one clue. I couldn't understand what had happened. I never left the road. Did I miss a street? Forget to turn? My logical mind kept saying, just turn around and go back, you'll eventually end up back where you started. I never did, yet somehow I eventually made my way home. And, while I thought I had been out for only thirty or forty minutes, I had been gone for over three hours! My friend, worried and wondering, had sent the kids out looking for me. Even odder, if someone was out running for over three hours, they would have covered a great deal of road. I did not, which is why I thought I'd only been out for a half-hour or so, and why I never thought to call. I didn't think anything was wrong.

Months later back home the memory of this popped up and I had this strange feeling that I had been transported somewhere else during my run. This would explain why I never left the road but had no idea where I was. That was all Spirit showed me in that moment, so I just figured that was the end of it. Fast forward seven years and I'm visiting my friend again. Prior to my trip, I began having dreams and visions of dragons; things would pop up out of nowhere with the word dragon or a picture of one, tattoos, figurines, you name it. Dragons were definitely making an appearance in my world. During my visit, we took a trip to a nearby bookstore and as I walked around the shop, I stopped in front of a shelf of spiritual self-help books and there, front and center, was a book on dragons and how to connect with them. Of course I bought it and jumped into it right away when I got back to the house. Later that day, I was scrolling my social media and the gal who facilitated my yoni steam sessions was advertising a special session with an activation to meet your dragon guide. Yep, you guessed it! That was what led me to meeting my beloved Lucille.

After I booked that appointment, I felt compelled to go for a walk down my mystery road that I loved so much. I decided to walk instead of run because I wanted to be very present and intentional. I wanted to connect with the energy of dragon and see if I could get some clarity on all my experiences. As I walked along the road, I mentally called out to the dragons, not really sure who I was asking for or knowing what to say. I had been connecting with Fae for so long that we'd become like old friends, but the dragon energy was new for me, making it feel a bit awkward at first. To be clear, Spirit in all forms is always happy and waiting for us to reach out. It doesn't matter who you're trying to reach or what words you use, they will receive your communication with love and are happy to make the connection with you. It's so important that you know and understand this. You cannot mess up working with Spirit. They are the most loving, forgiving energies in the Universe.

That day, they instantly heard my call and responded: *Yes, they said, you are correct. You were transported to another realm that day, the magical realm of dragon. In this space you were taught the ways of the keepers and the guardians, how to serve, how to protect, how to honor yourself, how to honor your voice, and even though you don't have any recollection of the experience, the teachings were imprinted in your DNA and you began living and behaving accordingly. We watched from above as you made new powerful decisions, spoke up more often and with fiery confidence, and finally began to love yourself as the powerful being you came here to be.*

And that, dear reader, is how I came to know and love dragons. There is a dragon guide waiting for you to reach out. They watch over you and protect you. When you are ready, they will hear your call. There is also a dragon living inside of you, that powerful presence that sees all, loves deeply, and guides you unconditionally through all the days of your life. How would it feel to meet that part of yourself? How would it feel to love that part of yourself? Are you willing to explore that?

FAERY TOOLBOX

This chapter is a collection of tools, practices, ideas and inspirations to help you connect with the Faery realm and in turn connect deeper to the source energy that lives inside of you.

Monday, September 27, 2021

I choose to tap into the miracle of all that I am and complete this manuscript today. I surrender to my voice, my magic, my purpose. I can do this. I release the need to distract myself with anything keeping me from my purpose. My commitment to this book is my priority until I check out tomorrow. I am magic. I am miracle. I am ready. Let's do this!

The above is a little pep talk I had with myself this morning before sitting down to write. One of the things I've learned from my guides is that we must be our own cheerleaders. Yes, we need friends, people we can confide in, receive support from, et cetera, but at the end of the day, all we is ourselves. People will inevitably disappoint and let us down, so we must be willing to hold that space for ourselves.

When I woke up this morning, I felt like I had hit a serious wall with this work. In my mind I could not take one more step. I was done. Suddenly my phone is buzzing. I look down and it's one of my most precious friends calling. I was still in bed and did not feel like doing a damn thing in that moment, but something told me to pick up the phone. As it turns out, she was exactly who I needed to speak to in that moment. My faery guides were moving through her in a wave of boisterous, celebratory cheers. My energy shifted almost immediately as I got out of bed and let her excitement soak into my being. We were on the phone less than five minutes, but it was more than enough time to kick me in the ass and get me moving again on my work. She reminded me of who I am and what I'm here to do. She knew exactly what to say and how it needed to be said. This is one of the ways the Fae will influence and guide you. They are here to oversee the work of the planet and if you have been called, they are not going to let you fail. This I promise you! Let's carry on, shall we?

One of the most beautiful things about working with the Faery realm is that even the simplest of things can be of value to the planet and show a commitment to the Fae that you are willing to step up and do the necessary work to help get this planet the love and respect it deserves. Things you may not even be aware of or realize just how important its impact is.

Pick up litter: This is one of the most powerful acts you can do to get the attention of Fae. Just look around your town and see the trash that people leave everywhere. It's disgusting and embarrassing and really shows how little we care about our planet. But you can help by picking up litter any chance you get. The Fae realize this is an enormous undertaking and do not expect you to do it all. This is where every little bit helps. Just do your part, even a single piece, is helpful. I know there have been many times I've been out and had the thought, *If only I had a bag to put it in, then I'd be happy to pick up some trash.* And not a moment after having that thought a plastic grocery bag will blow across my path, or I look over and there's one stuck inside a bush. This is Fae watching you, guiding you, seeing if you'll step up.

Donate and/or volunteer: Choose an environmental organization that speaks to your heart whose mission it is to help the planet in some way. If you've ever donated or volunteered for anything that moves you, you know how great it feels to give back to something that has your heart. If you've never experienced this before, give this one a try. You will be amazed at how great it feels to be of service in this way.

Plant flowers/trees/food: We live in a world where plant life is constantly being destroyed so that we can add more money to the bottom line of this life we've created. We are destroying the very resources we need to flourish on this planet. It only makes sense to give back in this way. You need not have a green thumb or lots of money to contribute in this way. It can be as small and simple as a single potted plant in a well-lit corner of your house. Plants clean the air helping you breathe better as well as brightening up any space, which in turn contributes to raising your vibration because you will feel this light each time you look on your plant. If you are in a position to go bigger with this, plant something that will enable you to share with others. This is a double win in the eyes of Fae. Sharing with others is always a great way to be of service. For example, if you're planting fruit trees, you immediately employ bees everywhere who are looking for work. This planet desperately needs more bees, and you know how I feel about bees – the more the better! And going back to the donate/volunteer option, if you choose an organization that provides education and resources on planting you can put even more energy into your endeavors.

Crystals: If you're anything like me you've been connecting with crystals and rocks since you were a child. I remember my grandfather taking me and my sister on road trips all over the state of Arizona. We'd always stop in any number of tourist shops where he would spoil us with trinkets and gifts. Every store we went into always had a large bin of tumbled stones of all shapes, sizes, and colors. I would find my way over there, dip my hands down to the bottom and just scoop them up and over, letting my hands play in the energy of them all. I couldn't stop touching them. On a conscious level, I didn't know they had magical, healing properties, but I know now that my spirit knew all about them. This is why I was always so attracted to them and had to touch them. I could feel their power even before I knew what it was. Crystals are a great place to start working with the Faery realm because they actually call to you. If you've never experienced working with the healing magic of crystals, just go into a shop and let yourself be guided by the ones that call you. You'll know because you are attracted to the color, the shape, even how it may feel in your hand. You may not be able to explain why you need this crystal, but you will purchase it anyway. By doing that, you're letting the Fae see that you're ready to begin learning the deeper properties of that which you chose, or that chose you. Let it be fun! Some great ones to begin with are rose quartz; amethyst; smoky quartz labradorite; black tourmaline; and citrine

Honestly, there are so many great ones, so again, lean toward the ones that are calling you. As you learn more, you will be guided to others. It's inevitable. As long as you are following your guidance, you cannot do this wrong.

Plant Medicine: This is an easy way to begin incorporating more "way of the fae" into your life, and it has been a magical addition to my world and my work with them. For me, the two most influential options are ceremonial cacao and essential oils. Ceremonial cacao is a sacred plant medicine used for centuries to open the heart and bring people back home to the sacred land and practices of their ancestors. It's consumed as a hot beverage and can be taken in community with others or as a solo ritual practice. Ceremonial cacao is a pretty recent addition to my practices; about ten months ago I attended a cacao ceremony. It was a potent, profound experience that shifted my life in incredible ways. I remember laughing when the gal facilitating the circle told me that cacao would make me quit my job, yet six months later that's exactly what I did.

I really cannot explain the magic of cacao. But when I sip it, somehow, I remember who I am before the world told me who I should be. It grounds me down to my bones and fills me with such gratitude and reverence for life. I weep almost every time I enjoy it. It's a potent magic that must be experienced to know and understand. When I am enjoying it on a regular basis, I make better choices with my food, my body, my life. It helps me not to drink wine when life is stressful. It is an extraordinary source of magnesium and if you're into having the best poops ever, then you've got to try it! Cacao is a non-hallucinogenic plant that creates a calm, gentle buzz inside the system. It's not caffeinated, therefore does not trigger the nervous system. It's a beautiful way to begin working with plant medicine.

Essential oils are my next favorite way to use plant medicine. Much like the crystals, essential oils will call out to you, as each has its own healing magic and vibrational imprint. Working with oils is another way to tune in deeper to your higher self and guidance from your spirit team. The more you do it, the stronger the communication becomes over time. Oils can be used topically with an appropriate carrier oil, as aromatherapy in a diffuser, or internally by adding to water or consuming as a capsule. As always, please research fully before taking anything internally, but also use this as an opportunity to go deeper into your intuition to see what your body is truly asking for. You may find it helpful to seek out a qualified herbalist to help clear up any questions or concerns you may have. Much of the work I do here is intuitive, but I still have to reach out to professionals who've studied these plants extensively so that I can better understand what I'm putting into my body. It's important that you trust yourself, but also not be afraid to reach out for help when you don't have all the answers.

Somatic dance: This is also something relatively new in my world, but it has made an enormous impact. Somatic dance is a way of getting back into your body through intuitive movement while surrendering control over what you think you look like or should be doing. In my experiences, I've always used a blindfold. I choose deep, soulful music and simply give my body permission to move however it sees fit. There is something magical that happens when you remove your sight and drop into the deep, feeling space of your body. Somatic dance is a way to release emotion from the body, any emotion. So while I choose slower, soulful music, to tap into the deep feels for myself, you may decide that faster, more intense music is what your body is calling for. Your body will tell you exactly what music needs to be heard and how it needs to be moved. Your only job here is to trust and surrender. My first experiences with somatic dance were done in a small group setting with others on a spiritual path. The facilitator also combined the experience with cacao, turning it into a potent and powerful ceremonial experience. If you are feeling self-conscious or nervous, you might consider adding in the heart-opening magic of ceremonial cacao. My favorite thing about somatic dance is how it taught me to feel so deeply and easily. It's a powerful modality that can move emotion quickly. I was even surprised that I could create just as powerful experiences at home dancing by myself. It was in this space that I felt the feeling of joy in my body for the very first time as an adult, at least that I was conscious of. I'm sure I've felt joy as a child, but when I felt that current move through my body at forty-six, I started to laugh and cry simultaneously. It was one of the most beautiful things I've ever felt. There was no mistaking it! I really hope that you give this a try. It's such a beautiful way to create a deeper, more loving relationship to yourself.

Sweeping outdoor areas: The Fae truly want us to know just how simple it can be to connect with their energy, and this is one of the ways they've guided me to them. Whenever I'm feeling uninspired, stuck or just plain out of sorts, I will sweep the doorway outside the front of my house. There is something magical that happens when you clear the energy that blocks the entrance to your home. I cannot explain it, you just have to try it! Once you get started, you will feel energized to keep going. Sweep other doorways, sidewalks, and pathways surrounding your home. As you do this give thanks to your body, your broom, your breath, give thanks for all you can see, smell, hear, and feel. Invite faery folk to join you. They are most certainly watching you, just waiting for you to reach out to them. If you have any bug messengers show up, welcome them in and give thanks for their presence. Even if you don't know what they're trying to say to you, acknowledging their presence lets them know you see them and honor them as part of the earthly journey. And if you are journaling regularly about your experiences, you will surely hear and know their messages in time as the pieces of your mystical puzzle begin to come together.

Sweeping has been a powerful way for me to move energy in my world. Because I am in my head a lot, the idea of sweeping, in its simplicity, is such a great way to get me moving. There's no way to overthink the act of sweeping. I've had so many beautiful things come to life simply by getting out of my own way, getting outside, and sweeping wherever I could. After coming inside, I suddenly had solutions to problems that had been weighing me down, phone calls would come in from clients wanting to book sessions, my mood would always be better – so many great things would happen, all just from sweeping the front doorway to my home.

As you begin to connect more with nature, you will be guided to your own ideas and inspiration to best impact your life. The important thing to remember in using any of these ideas or any ideas that are laid on your heart, is the importance of intention. You can create any sacred, nurturing practice with intention. You need only commit to being present and mindful in that which you wish to create. That is why something as simple as sweeping the front stoop can be such a potent, powerful act of connection to Source. And that's the beautiful thing about all of this, you have all the power. You truly do! Your intention, your mindfulness, your magic, can create miracles in your world. You need only believe in yourself, set your intentions, and commit to following through on the guidance when it's presented to you. This is how you create a spirit-led life.

THIS IS YOUR DREAM

If you made it this far into the world of Fae as seen through my eyes, the faery folk have their eye on you. Be sure of that! They are always recruiting new warriors of light to help love and care for this planet and Her people. If this scares you, take in a deep breath with me. You can do this! The faeries will guide you every step of the way. I promise you this. You will be given little assignments to build up your confidence and courage in this work. As you expand in your awareness and willingness to show up in greater ways, your assignments will expand as well.

You will never be alone on this path. Trust in that. Things will get weird, confusing, and possibly painful. Do not let this deter you from your path. Your work is so important and desperately needed now more than ever. Use this book to guide you, but also trust the guidance that comes through just for you. Your voice is going to grow stronger. You will no longer tolerate anything that is not in alignment with your highest self. The faeries are here to guide you back home to yourself. You will begin to see your place in this world as perfect and purposeful, no longer a random occurrence like you perhaps once believed. You have so much untapped power waiting to be discovered. This is your dream. You have the power to create the next stage of your life any way that you see fit. But you now understand that it's not just about you. Your dream affects the planet. You move now from a place of integrity and reverence. You love where you once feared. You now know and understand that what hurts one of us, hurts all of us. From this place of knowing, you make decisions that you know are for the greater good of all humankind.

This is honorable work. You are honoring your soul's purpose. Be proud of yourself. You are a warrior. Believe it. Claim it. Place a hand over your heart, close your eyes, and breathe in the truth of this. *Welcome home, Beloved, we've been waiting for you.*

ABOUT THE AUTHOR

Erin Christine is a Certified Transformational Life Coach, Licensed Massage Therapist specializing in Reflexology/Toe reading, and Reiki Master/Teacher. For almost two decades she has traveled within and around the spirit realms, navigating life as a clairvoyant, clairaudient, and empath. She uses the power of storytelling and elements of nature to empower curious, playful women to fully embody their unique voices and connect deeply to her spirits.

Erin has experienced a curious, unusual life that has been fraught with sexual and emotional abuse, chronic pain, and unexplained health issues. She discovered the secrets to her healing could be found by connecting deeply with nature after being introduced to her spirit guides, the faeries, in 2002. This awakening has impacted Erin's life in unimaginable ways. A storyteller, seer, poet, and magician, she weaves her own world, breathing in a balance of human suffering and alchemy. She sees beyond the veil and feels the world's pain. This gift has granted her access to the deepest parts of herself and has led her to her sacred work.

A self-proclaimed nature coach, Erin is more of a tree-hugging, dirt-loving, bug whisperer who's constantly on the lookout for the greatest treehouse ever created to live out the rest of her days.

Connect with Erin Christine:

www.erinchristine.org

www.facebook.com/erin.ockenfels

Private group: www.facebook.com/groups/bornthisfae

Instagram: www.instagram.com/sunshinemama333

Other published work ~ *The Wild Woman's Book of Shadows:*
www.erinchristine.org/shop

Acknowledgments

A lifetime of gratitude and appreciation for my mom Amy Jo for having the courage to say yes to my life long before anyone else was ready for me. Your brave became my brave. Thank you from the whole of my heart for always having faith in me and supporting my work. I am because you are. I love you.

To my dad in Heaven, Gary, you were my very first, and greatest, teacher. Your fear taught me to love, and for that I am forever grateful. I feel you beaming down on me, and I know that I have made you proud. I love you, Dad.

To my exceptional sister, Carrie Amanda. I have survived a ridiculous life because you stood by me and made me laugh, deep, hard, healing belly laughs that I know were the magic I needed to pull myself from the darkness. Thank you for never giving up on me.

To my beautiful daughter Savannah Faith, your inner fire and unwavering faith in yourself gives me the courage to dig deeper into this life and show up as the woman I always hoped I'd be. You woke me up. The strength in my spirit, the fire in my voice, and the love in my being all exist because of you. This book is a tribute to you, baby girl. Thank you.

To Gina Angelini, for twenty-seven years of talk, tears,

and laughter. This book wouldn't be here without your sacred counsel. You've held my hand, my heart, and allowed me to ascend as I needed to, always there to catch me if I fell. Dr. Scholls in sync, soul sister – here's to the next twenty-seven!

To the abundant and extraordinary list of teachers and mentors who have all shown up in perfect, divine time for my expansion. I thank you from the whole of my heart for your guidance, your wisdom, and the courage to walk through the fires of your own self-discovery so that I may one day learn from you. A special thank you to Sunny Dawn Johnston, Melissa Kim Corter, Cheryl Speen, Jamie Bishop, and Jan Nichols, who took me into deep healing places that terrified me, only to lift me up and show me the light of my own being. Massive love and gratitude to you all!

To my sacred soul family, my tribe of ride-or-die peeps, you know who you are. I love you, I honor you, and I thank you for always showing me the best in myself.

To Shanda Trofe and the team at Transcendent Publishing, thank you for your presence, your counsel, and all the ways you bring my magic to life. I am honored and blessed to walk this journey with you.

And finally, to my Father God, Holy Mother, Beloved angels, ancestors, and guides, thank you for your tireless faith in me and keeping me on track when I wanted to run away. Thank you for trusting me with this message, giving me courage to claim it as my own, and showing me how to share it best with the world.